FORTRESS • 107

DEFENSE OF THE THIRD REICH 1941–45

STEVEN J ZALOGA

ILLUSTRATED BY ADAM HOOK

Series editor Marcus Cowper

First published in 2012 by Osprey Publishing,
Midland House, West Way, Botley, Oxford OX2 0PH, UK
43-01 21st Street, Suite 220B, Long Island City, NY 11101, USA

Email: info@ospreypublishing.com

© 2012 Osprey Publishing Limited

Osprey Publishing is part of the Osprey Group.

Print ISBN: 978 1 84908 593 9
PDF e-book ISBN: 978 1 84908 594 6
EPUB e-book ISBN: 978 1 78200 303 8

Editorial by Ilios Publishing Ltd, Oxford, UK (www.iliospublishing.com)
Cartography by Bounford.com
Page layout by Ken Vail Graphic Design, Cambridge, UK (kvgd.com)
Typeset in Myriad and Sabon
Index by Judy Oliver
Originated by PDQ Digital Media Solutions, Suffolk UK
Printed in China through Bookbuilders

13 14 15 16 17   11 10 9 8 7 6 5 4 3 2

A CIP catalog record for this book is available from the British Library.

www.ospreypublishing.com

ARTIST'S NOTE

Readers may care to note that the original paintings from which the color plates in this book were prepared are available for private sale. All reproduction copyright whatsoever is retained by the Publishers. All enquiries should be addressed to:

Scorpio, 158 Mill Road, Hailsham, East Sussex BN27 2SH, UK
scorpiopaintings@btinternet.com

The Publishers regret that they can enter into no correspondence upon this matter.

THE FORTRESS STUDY GROUP (FSG)

The object of the FSG is to advance the education of the public in the study of all aspects of fortifications and their armaments, especially works constructed to mount or resist artillery. The FSG holds an annual conference in September over a long weekend with visits and evening lectures, an annual tour abroad lasting about eight days, and an annual Members' Day.

The FSG journal *FORT* is published annually, and its newsletter *Casemate* is published three times a year. Membership is international. For further details, please contact:
secretary@fsgfort.com
Website: www.fsgfort.com

THE HISTORY OF FORTIFICATION STUDY CENTER (HFSC)

The History of Fortification Study Center (HFSC) is an international scientific research organization that aims to unite specialists in the history of military architecture from antiquity to the 20th century (including historians, art historians, archeologists, architects and those with a military background). The Center has its own scientific council, which is made up of authoritative experts who have made an important contribution to the study of fortification.

The HFSC's activities involve organizing conferences, launching research expeditions to study monuments of defensive architecture, contributing to the preservation of such monuments, arranging lectures and special courses in the history of fortification and producing published works such as the refereed academic journal *Questions of the History of Fortification*, monographs and books on the history of fortification. It also holds a competition for the best publication of the year devoted to the history of fortification.

The headquarters of the HFSC is in Moscow, Russia, but the Center is active in the international arena and both scholars and amateurs from all countries are welcome to join. More detailed information about the HFSC and its activities can be found on the website: www.hfsc.3dn.ru

E-mail: ciif-info@yandex.ru

THE WOODLAND TRUST

CONTENTS

DEFENSE OF THE THIRD REICH 1940–45

INTRODUCTION

From 1940 to 1945, Germany was subjected to the most intense aerial bombing campaign to date, totalling some two million tons of bombs. Germany's response to the Allied air attacks was a mix of active and passive air defense tactics, including fighter aircraft, Flak, and air-raid protection. An important but often overlooked aspect of these air defense efforts was an associated fortification program. The Luftwaffe's lavishly equipped Flak force is well known, but its methods of deployment and use of field works is detailed here for the first time. The largest single fortification effort inside Germany during the war was a program to create air-raid bunkers and other forms of shelters, an effort four times the size of the Maginot Line construction program. In the final year of the war, Germany attempted to shield its most vital factories from air attack by an urgent scheme to construct underground and fortified factories. Although now forgotten, the Third Reich's air defense fortification program was intensely studied by the Allies after the war and served as the inspiration for many Cold War bunker programs.

The LVZ-West fortification program in the late 1930s in the Saar included numerous command posts such as this LVZ-K bunker, variously designated as a *Kommandostand* or *Gefechtsstand*. This bunker was typically used as a Flak battalion command post and was designed to accommodate 24 troops. It was 16m (52ft) wide, 8m (26ft) deep and used 455 cubic metres (600,000 cubic yards) of concrete. (Library of Congress)

The early Flak field works tended to be simple earthen berms around the guns. This is an example of an 88mm Flak G-Stand as displayed in the 1939 Luftwaffe manual for Flak emplacements. (NARA)

FLAK EMPLACEMENTS

Pre-war Luftwaffe Flak

Until the mid-1930s, the Flak force had been controlled by the army (Heer) and was primarily oriented towards the tactical defense of the field army. When Hitler renounced the Versailles treaty and created the independent Luftwaffe in March 1935, its new commander, Hermann Göring, took steps to absorb the Flak force into the new Luftwaffe. This was the first step in a process that would eventually see the Luftwaffe assume the primary responsibility for air defense of the Third Reich.

As part of this process, the Luftwaffe embarked on a major rearmament effort that included the acquisition of about 1,900 88mm heavy Flak guns, along with associated gun directors, sound detectors and searchlights. The 88mm heavy Flak gun became the basis for national air defense, supplemented by 20mm and 37mm light Flak guns for low-altitude defense. The air campaigns of the Spanish Civil War in 1936–39 were intensely studied for lessons regarding the air defense of cities and the value of Flak in modern warfare.

The first major investment in fixed Flak positions for national air defense was part of the larger Westwall fortification effort. By the late 1930s, the principal bomber threat was the French Armée de l'Air, and the Westwall program included the Air Defense Zone-West (LVZ-West, or Luftverteidigungszone West). This created a Flak belt stretching from the Eifel region, south through the Saar along the Mosel River, and on to the Black Forest and Swiss frontier. The LVZ-West was not intended to present an impenetrable wall, but rather to act as an initial barrier to French or British bomber attack that would identify the direction of the attack and disrupt it before it could reach its intended target zones deeper in Germany. The initial line consisted of light Flak batteries armed with 20mm and 37mm guns, followed by a second line armed with heavy 88mm guns. Serious construction began in 1938 and was supervised by a special staff of Flak-Regiment 29 in Frankfurt-am-Rhein. In total, 2,056 bunkers were built for LVZ-West from Düren to Karlsruhe through the summer of 1940 at 48 light Flak and 197 heavy Flak sites capable of accommodating 576 light Flak guns and 788 88mm Flak guns. The LVZ-West contained about a third of the heavy Flak batteries available at the start of the war.

The LVZ-West construction was based on seven standard designs. These included command posts (F-Stand, or *Führerstand*, G-Stand, or

One of the standard configurations for Flak emplacements was the use of a parapet around the G-Stand with outer walls of planks and the space between filled with earth. The ammunition lockers for this 37mm Flak gun were located around the periphery of the gun pit, while one of the lockers was set aside for equipment associated with the gun. This particular emplacement of the 4. Flak-Division was captured by the US 7th Armored Division on the Edersee in the Hesse region in late March 1945. (NARA)

Gefechtsstand), ammunition bunkers (M-Stand, or *Munitionsraum*), and personnel shelters (U-Raum, or *Doppelgruppenunterstand*); V-Stand (*Gruppenunterstand am Voderhang*), as well as defensive types such as small machine-gun posts. As will be noted, none of the standardized bunkers were designed to accommodate the Flak guns. Instead, the guns were deployed in less expensive earthen fieldworks. The presumption was that the Flak sites were not likely to be primary targets, and that personnel and ammunition were more vulnerable than the guns. Luftwaffe tactical doctrine recognized that there would never be enough Flak guns to cover every possible objective, and so the 88mm heavy Flak gun was designed to be mobile; batteries could be shifted to respond to the objectives of enemy bombing campaigns.

The LVZ-West was the first attempt to create an integrated air defense system incorporating sensors such as searchlights and sound detectors, a common air reporting system, as well as Flak guns and fighter bases. Although the 1937 Luftwaffe armament program included funding for air defense radar, this new technology did not play a major role in the LVZ-West.

At the beginning of the war, the Luftwaffe Flak force was the most lavishly equipped in the world. There were 2,628 heavy Flak guns (88mm and 105mm) compared to about 1,300 heavy anti-aircraft guns in Britain. Although the Luftwaffe was responsible for both strategic air defense of the

When Flak batteries were re-positioned in 1944, they often ended up in improvised emplacements. This is a reinforced G-Stand for a 88mm heavy Flak gun of the 7. Flak-Division stationed near Neuss and captured by the Ninth US Army in March 1945 during the fighting along the Rhine. The emplacement has brick walls, and the ammunition lockers are of improvised construction using sections of concrete drainage pipe. The gun is typical of wartime static Flak units, with a simple *Sockellafette* mount. (NARA)

An 88mm heavy Flak gun in an enhanced G-Stand with the outer walls made of poured-concrete. This gun is an early example that is still mounted on the mobile cruciform base; most Flak emplacements deployed after 1941 used a simple *Sockellafette* pedestal mount. (NARA)

Reich and tactical air defense of the army, in 1939 about 80 percent of its resources were devoted to homeland defense. The one area where Britain had a significant lead was in its integrated air defense system which included the Chain Home radars and a sophisticated network of forward observers and air reporting centres which collated the data and passed it on to both the fighter and AA gun force. Germany had begun to take steps in this direction, but it had not integrated early warning radars into its network as extensively as in Britain. In late 1939, the Luftwaffe had only eight Freya early warning radars on the German Bight, the small stretch of coastline along the North Sea between the Netherlands and Denmark that was especially vulnerable to British bomber attack.

Acceleration of air defense in 1940

With the start of the war in September 1939, German cities were subjected to air defense decrees such as mandatory night-time black outs. The RAF launched its first bomber attack against the Wilhelmshaven naval base on September 4, 1940. Britain and France refrained from bomber attacks on German cities during the Phoney War from September 1939 to May 1940. The French Armée de l'Air conducted nearly a thousand night missions into Germany during the Phoney War, but they were primarily reconnaissance and leaflet missions. Likewise, RAF bombers were confined to leaflet raids and a limited number of attacks on German military targets, especially shipping. British anti-shipping raids in December 1939 were hotly received and Flak along the coast proved so effective that instructions were issued to avoid low-level attacks and conduct missions from 13,000 feet. Some Allied air attacks during the Battle of France in May–June 1940 struck German cities along the border, but were aimed at military objectives. Although Germany bombed cities such as Warsaw in 1939 and Rotterdam in 1940, the Luftwaffe refrained from attacks on major French and British cities due to the concern that it would unleash an unrestrained bomber campaign.

In the event, an inadvertent German raid on London during the initial phase of the Battle of Britain in August 1940 prompted Churchill to authorize retaliatory strikes against Berlin. Berlin was first hit on the night of August 25–26, 1940 and Hitler then unleashed an intensified campaign against British cities. The restraint shown in the first year of the war evaporated,

Luftwaffe Flak batteries in Germany			
	Heavy gun	Light gun	Searchlight
Jan. 1941	537	395	138
Jan. 1942	744	438	174
Jan. 1943	628	535	277
Dec. 1943	1,300	708	395
Feb. 1944	1,508	623	375
Aug. 1944	2,655	1,602	470

and German cities quickly became a target of the RAF. The first few raids on Berlin in August 1940 were small scale and mainly hit the city's outskirts. Their psychological and political consequences, however, were far greater.

Göring had boasted that Berlin would never be bombed, but it became blatantly clear that Berlin was no longer inviolate. The persistence of the British raids into September 1940 forced the Nazi Party to react. On September 9, 1940, Hitler ordered the construction of six Flak tower complexes in Berlin. The Berlin Flak towers were emblematic of Hitler's architectural enthusiasms, and were the most massive fortified structures yet undertaken by Nazi Germany. The designs were in the neo-Romantic style favoured by Hitler, with an attempt to incorporate details of medieval fortresses. The location of the massive Flak positions in central Berlin were intended to reassure German civilians of the impregnable defenses of the Reich. Details of these structures are covered later in the section on air-raid bunkers.

The increasing threat of RAF bomber attack in 1940–42 accelerated the growth of heavy Flak in the homeland defense role. In September 1939, Luftwaffe Flak deployed 2,628 heavy Flak guns in the 88mm–105mm range, and by February 1944 this grew more than five-fold to 13,500 heavy guns. In general, more than half of the heavy Flak guns were located in Germany for air defense of the Reich, with the remainder being deployed in other theatres for both tactical defense of the field armies as well as regional defense of key installations. The Flak batteries based in Germany were often dubbed *Heimatflak* (Homeland Flak).

Integrated air defense

The early air battles over the Reich in 1940–41 were a struggle of the blind against the blind. Early RAF attempts to conduct daylight bombing raids into Germany were savaged by the Luftwaffe fighter force, and the RAF switched to night-bombing. The early campaigns in 1941 were directed against industry and transportation targets, but the lack of night navigation and bombing aids resulted in such poor accuracy that the attacks were often worthless. The German Flak force had been developed primarily to deal with

The 128mm Flak 40 was the best heavy Flak gun in German service during the war and began to enter service in 1942. It was not especially numerous, with only 570 in service by 1945. This shows a typical enhanced G-Stand using brick construction for the walls of the gun pit. The ammunition lockers in the wall are numbered, which was standard Luftwaffe practice. This particular gun belonged to the 14. Flak-Division defending the Leuna refinery. This division claimed the destruction of 147 American tanks during the fighting in this sector in April 1945, mainly against the US 2nd Armored Division. (NARA)

the threat posed by daylight attacks, and relied on an elementary air alert system. Visual observers were stationed at Fluwa (Flugwach) posts and telephoned their reports to an area Fluko (*Flugwachekommando*, or air reporting centre). This data was used to alert neighbouring Flak units. Long-range early warning was conducted by the handful of Freya early warning radars along the German Bight and a network of outmoded sound detectors.

This early warning network expanded in 1940–41 as more radars were manufactured, and was gradually extended along the coastline of occupied Europe, especially in France, Belgium, the Netherlands, and Denmark. For night combat, Flak units within Germany originally relied on sound-detectors (RHH, or *Ringtrichter-Richtungshörer*) to aim their searchlights, but the inherent inaccuracies of such a system, along with the difficulties of using optical gun directors at night resulted in abysmal accuracy. Indeed, the poor accuracy of the heavy guns at night forced the use of crude tactics such as barrage fire. This was both wasteful of expensive ammunition, and ineffective. The Luftwaffe was also slow to embrace radar-equipped night-fighters, in no small measure due to the unsophisticated notions of senior leadership such as Göring and Ernst Udet, the head of the Luftwaffe technical office. Udet once complained that radar "took the fun out of flying."

The 128mm anti-aircraft was also built in a twin mount, but only 33 were deployed by 1945 as the 128mm Flakzwilling 40. They were used principally on the Flak towers in Berlin, Hamburg and Vienna as this example is seen here on Gefechtstürm IV in the Heiligengeistfeld area of Hamburg with the spire of St Michael's church evident in the background. (NARA)

A vital first step in improving the night-fighter force was taken in the summer of 1940 when the scattered units were consolidated into NJG 1 (*Nachtjagdgeschwader*, "night-fighter wing") under Oberst Josef Kammhuber. This talented young officer saw his responsibilities greatly expand through 1941 as it became apparent that Germany required an integrated air defense network comparable to that in Britain. The shortcomings in German aircraft-mounted night-fighter radars forced Kammhuber to shift his attention to ground-based means, first by deploying a *Scheinwerfer-Riegel* ("searchlight belt") along the German frontier, alerted and directed by Freya early warning radars and sound-detector. The belt consisted of a line of rectangles 45km (2 miles) wide and 22km (14 miles) deep, codenamed *Himmelbett* ("four-poster bed"), each with their own control post. The *Himmelbett* system was based initially on *Henaja* tactics (*Helle Nachtjagd*, "illuminated night-fighting") which used the radars and sound detectors to locate an approaching RAF bomber and direct a master searchlight against it, followed by nearby searchlights. The night-fighters assigned to each *Himmelbett* sector could then attack the intruding bombers using the searchlight illumination. The RAF dubbed this belt the "Kammhuber Line" after its commander. By the late summer of 1941, there were enough of the new Würzburg radars available so that much more sophisticated *Dunaja* tactics (*Dunkle Nachtjad*, "dark night fighting") could be used in the *Himmelbett* sectors. Each *Himmelbett* sector contained a Freya early warning radar and two of the more precise Würzburg radars. The Freya would detect the approach of British bombers, one Würzburg would track the bombers, while the second Würzburg would

track the German night-fighters. Data from the radars went to a *Himmelbett* night-fighter control station that passed the data to the night-fighters. The searchlights were moved back further east, so that if the radar direction failed to conclude the interception, the searchlight belt and Flak guns behind the radar line could have another try.

This system was originally limited to the forward-deployed night-fighter units, but gradually a number of the most vulnerable German cities were covered using *Konaja* integrated air defense tactics (from *Kombinierte Nachtjagd*) which provided targeting data to both Flak and night-fighter units. These networks had central command posts codenamed Kiebitz (Kiel), Hummel (Hamburg), Roland (Bremen), Drössel (Ruhr region), Kolibri (Cologne), Dachs Nord (Frankfurt), Dachs Sud (Mannheim), Mücke (Munich) and Bärs (Berlin). This marked the start of the introduction of radars into the Flak force.

The Kammhuber Line underwent continual amplification and improvements through 1943. In the spring of 1942, the new Würzburg-Riese ("giant Wurzburg") was introduced which offered significantly improved range. New long-range early warning radars including a Freya-derivative, the Mammut ("mammoth"), were deployed along the Channel coast to identify the RAF bombers at the earliest possible opportunity and alert the *Himmelbett* stations. The story of the development of German air defense radar is far too complicated to be detailed here, but it had an immediate impact on air defense fortification efforts. To begin with, the creation of the Kammhuber Line initiated an extensive construction program in France, Belgium, the Netherlands, and Denmark. This consisted of numerous radar sites, control posts, and the *Himmelbett* command posts. In the case of the forward-deployed radars along

Luftwaffe defense of the Reich, 1944

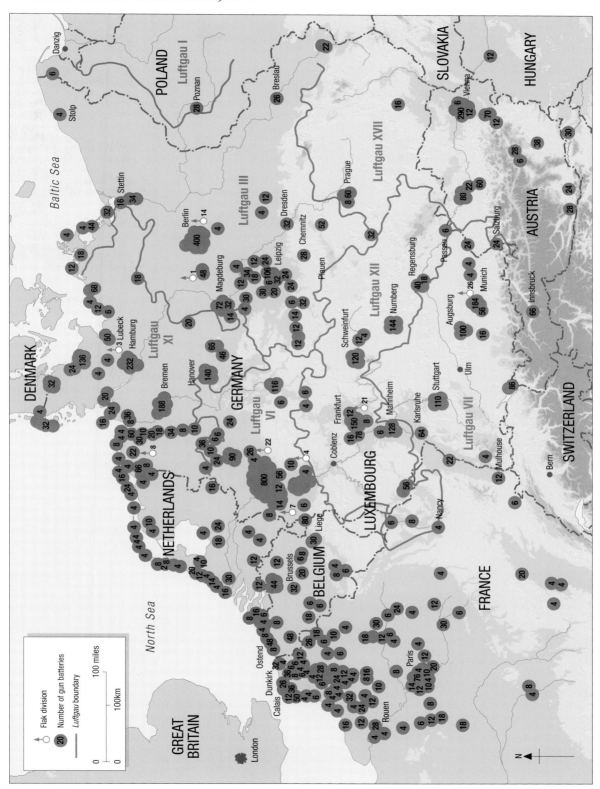

RRH (*Ringtrichter-Richtungshörer*) sound detectors were the standard method of aiming searchlights in the early-war years until the advent of fire-control radars. This RHH is crewed by Luftwaffe Flakhelferinnen, the women's auxiliary service which took over an increasing part of the Flak arm's signals and communication posts as a way to free up manpower for other combat arms. (Library of Congress)

the coast, the radar posts became enveloped in the Atlantikwall fortification effort that was gathering steam by 1942. Instead of simple tactical emplacements, the radars were erected in fully protected bunker complexes consisting of a fortified radar post along with associated shelters for the crews. The construction of these Luftwaffe sites consumed about 10 percent of the material used in the construction of the Atlantikwall in 1943–44.[1]

Besides the radar sites themselves, a network of command sites was gradually erected as well. Each radar site had an associated command post (*Flugmeldemess-Stellung*), originally located in a simple wooden building called a "T-hut" due to its shape. Some radar sites, especially those along the Atlantikwall, altered from simple T-huts to standard L487 concrete bunkers in 1942–44. Radar sites would pass their information along to the regional command centre, originally known as the NaFü (*Nachtjagdraumführer*, "night-fighter director"). With the increasing tempo of US Army Air Force daylight bomber attacks in 1943, the early warning system switched from a night-time to an all-day system and the command centres were redesignated as JaFü (*Jagdabschnittsführer*, "fighter sector director"). These posts were generally located in extremely large, well-protected bunkers called *Zentralgefechtsstanden* ("central battle stations").

Flak expansion

As RAF bombing attacks against Germany increased in 1941–42, heavy Flak guns were deployed for Reich air defense outside Germany along the "Bomber Autobahn," the main air routes between Britain and Germany over the Netherlands and Belgium. At its peak in 1943–44, about 70 percent of the Luftwaffe heavy Flak batteries were involved in air defense of the Reich, either in Germany itself, or in the western approaches in the Low Countries.

Although the Luftwaffe attempted to monopolize the control of large Flak units, the Kriegsmarine eventually created its own units, ostensibly limited to the protection of German ports. This force expanded greatly during the war, eventually numbering 88 *Marine Flak-Abteilungen*, each with four to six batteries. Many of the Flak batteries on the approaches to the Reich along the Dutch coast were Kriegsmarine batteries. Both the Heer (army) and Waffen-SS also organized Flak units during the war, but these were small tactical formations, usually organic to divisions and not used for homeland defense.

The Luftwaffe's homeland air defense artillery force was organized in large formations, generally divisions and brigades, which were subordinate to the local Luftwaffe regional commands, the *Luftgau*. The Flak division was

[1] For further details and the Atlantic Wall see: Steven Zaloga, *The Atlantic Wall (1): France* (Osprey Fortress 63, 2007) and *The Atlantic Wall (2): Belgium, the Netherlands, Denmark, and Norway* (Osprey Fortress 89, 2009).

The brains of the Flak battery was its gun director which combined an optical range finder with a ballistic computer to provide the battery's guns with precise firing solutions. The standard type during the war was the Kommandogerät 40, seen here in service with the 26. Flak-Division outside Munich. (MHI)

the basic tactical formation and was usually a regional organization with a flexible structure to manage all Flak sub-units within a given area. Typically, the division was broken into Flak groups (*Gruppen*), with the group's headquarters assigned to defend a specific area. The group headquarters was comparable to a regimental headquarters in size. The group was in turn broken down into sector sub-groups (*Untergruppen*) with a headquarters roughly battalion-sized. A large city would typically have several groups; Munich for example, was defended by three heavy groups (Gruppen Nord-Ost, Nord-West and Sud) divided into five *Untergruppen*, a light sub-group with five *Untergruppen*, and elements of Scheinwerfer-Regiment 8, all subordinate to the 26. Flak-Division of Luftgau VII.

Through the course of the war, German Flak batteries came to depend on fire-control radars on a scale of two per battery. This is a Telefunken FuMG 41 T Mannheim radar, later called the FuMG 64 in use with the 26. Flak-Division near Munich in 1945. (MHI)

The basic combat formation for Flak was the gun battery (*Batterie*). At the start of the war, German heavy Flak batteries had four guns each. During the 1940–41 fighting, it became evident that the four-gun batteries were not sufficiently lethal against British bombers. As a first step, batteries were expanded to six guns, and this eventually became the common battery composition for most of the war. In the autumn of 1941, there were experiments with eight-gun double batteries (*Doppelbatterien*) and with 12-gun triple batteries (*Dreifach-Batterien*). These experiments were not entirely successful, and in particular the 12-gun battery was viewed as uneconomical due to its reliance on poor fire control data from a single command post.

Due to RAF reliance on night tactics in 1940–44, searchlights played a major role in German air defense. Searchlight regiments (*Scheinwerfer-Regimenten*) were generally under divisional control, and their subordinate battalions and batteries were scattered through the Flak division's operating area, ideally on a scale of a battalion per Flak group and a battery per sub-group. Searchlights also played an important role in illuminating British night bombers for the German night-fighter force, and so they were often deployed independently of the Flak batteries for this mission, for example in the Scheinwerfer Riegel as mentioned earlier.

The principal innovation in Flak fire control in 1941 was the introduction of fire-control radars, first with the Würzburg and then with dedicated gun-control radars such as the Funkmessgerät. 39 (FuMG. 39) and the later FuMG. 41. By March 1942, about a third of the heavy Flak batteries had a radar. There were not enough radars to go around, so the practice began of concentrating the normal batteries into super-batteries (*Grossbatterien*) with the individual battery command posts consolidated into centralized operations centres (*Auswertungen*) to coordinate and concentrate their fire. The Grossbatterien were usually placed on the bomber approach routes and likely bombing lines, but outside the target area. The heavy gun batteries with the newer 105mm Flak guns were given priority for this configuration. In 1942, there were experiments with even larger batteries, nicknamed the "Mammoths" (*Mammutenbatterien*), which contained 36 guns.

One of the most common air search radars in use to support the Flak force during 1942–45 was the FuMG 65 Würzburg-Riese, better known by the Allied intelligence designation "Wurzburg Giant". This system weighed 11 metric tons and so was usually mounted in a static position. This particular radar from the 4. Flak-Division was located near Bad Godesburg in 1945. (NARA)

Flak dispositions in the Munich area, 1945

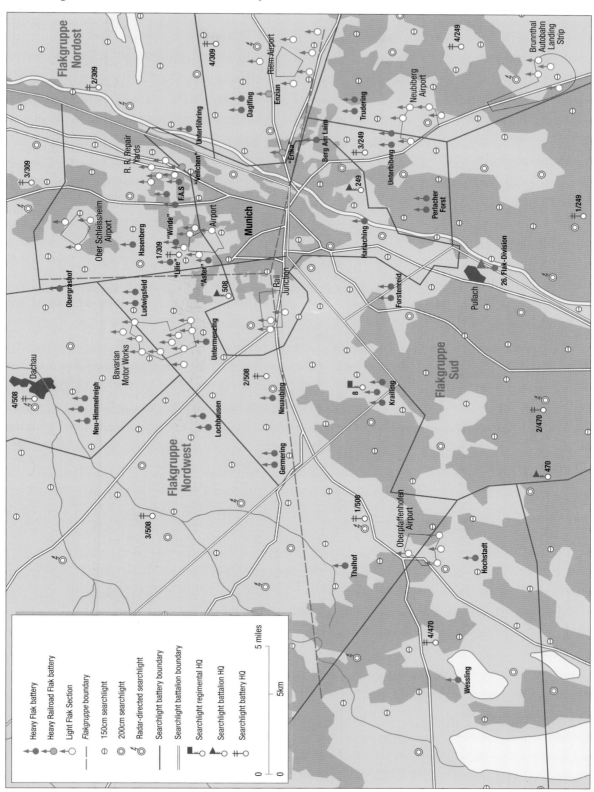

Flakgruppe Nordost

Flakgruppe Nordwest

Flakgruppe Sud

2/309

4/309

Rem Airport

Enzian

"Erika"

4/249

Brunnthal Autobahn Landing Strip

3/309

Daglfing

Unterföhring

Trudering

Neubiberg Airport

Berg Am Laim

3/249

R. R. Repair Yards

"Veilchen"

249

Unterbiberg

"Winde"

F.A.S

Munich

Perlacher Forst

Ober Schleissheim Airport

Airport

Hasenberg

1/309

"Lilie"

"Aster"

508

Hataching

1/249

Obergrashof

Ludwigsfeld

Rail Junction

Forstenried

26. Flak-Division

Pullach

Bavarian Motor Works

Untermenzing

Dachau

4/508

Neu-Himmelreigh

Lochhausen

2/508

Neuaubing

8

Kralling

Flakgruppe Sud

2/470

Germering

470

3/508

Oberpfaffenhofen Airport

1/508

Hochstadt

Thalhof

4/470

Wessling

Legend

Heavy Flak battery
Heavy Railroad Flak battery
Light Flak Section
Flakgruppe boundary
150cm searchlight
200cm searchlight
Radar-directed searchlight
Searchlight battery boundary
Searchlight battalion boundary
Searchlight regimental HQ
Searchlight battalion HQ
Searchlight battery HQ

5 miles

5km

0

0

This is the suggested layout for a six-gun heavy Flak battery from the October 1943 manual. The heavy gun battery (1) includes six gun-pits (G: *Gefechtsstand*) along with associated underground ammunition shelters (M: *Munitionsunterschlupf*) connected by trenches, as well as underground crew shelters (U: *Unterkunft*). On a hill to the right is a three-gun light flak section (2) to provide protection for the main battery; it has a similar arrangement of munition and crew shelters. The battery fire control centre (3) includes the command post (BS: *Befehlsstand*); two radars (FuMG: *Funkmeßgerät*), and gun director (KG: *Kommandogerät*) and two dugouts for associated power generator trailers (MS: *Maschinensatzschuppen*). The site measures approximately 320m wide (1,000ft) by 120m (400ft) deep.

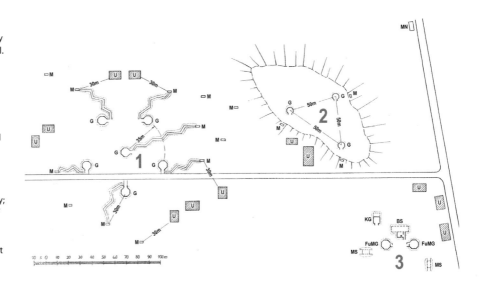

Even after the advent of radars, sound detectors were never completely abandoned, because of the shortage of radar equipment. Sound detectors were revived after the summer of 1943 when the RAF began introducing effective anti-radar tactics using "Window" jamming strips. So there were still 5,560 sound detectors in service in 1944.

Reich defense forces had large numbers of light Flak guns in the 20mm and 37mm range, but they played a minor role in defending the Reich against air attack in 1941–44 since the bombers usually attacked from altitudes outside their range. Light Flak remained useful in tactical air defense, and so surplus batteries were redeployed outside Germany. There was a short revival of light Flak from mid-1944 to 1945 due to the increasing number of Allied fighters engaging in strafing missions, and this issue will be discussed in more detail below.

Although Luftwaffe Flak doctrine stressed the need for mobility, industrial shortcuts through the war forced the heavy Flak into static deployments. The cruciform platform and associated transport caissons that were fitted to pre-war Flak guns were expensive to manufacture, and were usually idle at most Flak sites for years at a time. As a result, by 1942, the Flak industry dropped the cruciform mounts for home defense Flak guns in favour of a simple pedestal mount (*Sockellafette*) especially for the heavy 105mm and 128mm guns and Göring formally ordered this switch in June 1942.

While static gun batteries were more economical, there was still the need for a mobile reserve. Allied bombing campaigns in 1943–44 often switched their focus from one city or region to another, and so some static Flak units were overwhelmed, while at the same time neighbouring units were entirely idle. This issue had been recognized even before the war, and led to the creation of the first ten railway Flak batteries (*Eisenbahn-Flak*). The growing need for this mobile reserve force increased after the June 1942 decision to deploy most of the Flak in static positions, so plans were drawn up to deploy 100 railroad batteries by 1943. It was originally hoped to base this on heavier calibre 105mm and 128mm guns, but in the end, all three common heavy Flak guns were used, the 88mm, 105mm and 128mm. About 50 railroad batteries were deployed by 1942, and 100 by 1943. Priority for railroad batteries was given to industrial zones, and secondly to major railway marshalling yards.

Flak emplacements

Heavy Flak guns deployed in the air defense of the Reich were based mainly in static entrenchments. The design of the Flak emplacements was overseen by the Fortification Unit of the Inspectorate for Flak Artillery (Insp. der Flakartillerie-Abteilung Befestigung). Luftwaffe Flak tactics recognized three principal modes of Flak emplacement: basic (*einfache*), reinforced (*verstärkte*) and enhanced (*erweitere*). The basic emplacement (*einfache Feldstellung*) offered an elementary form of temporary protection that could be constructed by the battery's own crews using simple and readily available material. Through the late 1930s, the Luftwaffe manuals recommended a simple earth berm, but by 1940, more elaborate structures were recommended. One 1940 option suggested a parapet around the gun consisting of two parallel walls of wood planking with the space between filled with earth or gravel. The 1943 manual suggested simpler construction using a single wooden plank wall with earth packed against the outside. Flak units seldom used camouflage nets as they interfered with gun readiness and there was little concern that homeland Flak batteries would be targeted.

The reinforced emplacement (*verstärkte Feldstellung*) used more robust construction material and had a larger and more complex layout. This type of emplacement had concrete over the crew quarters and munitions lockers and so was intended to offer better protection against air attack. Although log construction was the most common configuration, this type of emplacement could also substitute concrete or brick construction when available. These type of emplacements were often built with the assistance of specialized Luftwaffe construction units.

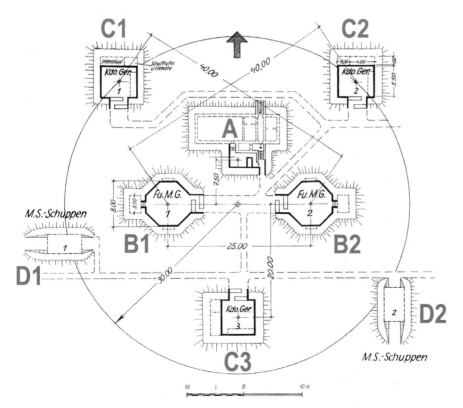

This is the suggested layout for a *Grossbatterie* command centre (*Befehlsstelle*) from the October 1943 Luftwaffe manual. This particular configuration is for a three-gun battery; a two-gun battery would have only two Kdo.Ger. 40 and a one-gun battery only one. The site is approximately 60m (200ft) in diameter. The command post A (*Befelsstand*) is in the centre of the position and the arrow points in the direction of main command post. The two radar fire-direction posts (B1 and B2) are located behind the command post. Around the periphery of the site are the three Kommandogerät 40 gun directors, one dedicated to each battery (C1-C3). There are also two entrenchments (D1, D2) for associated power generator trailers (*Maschinensatz Schuppen* or MS).

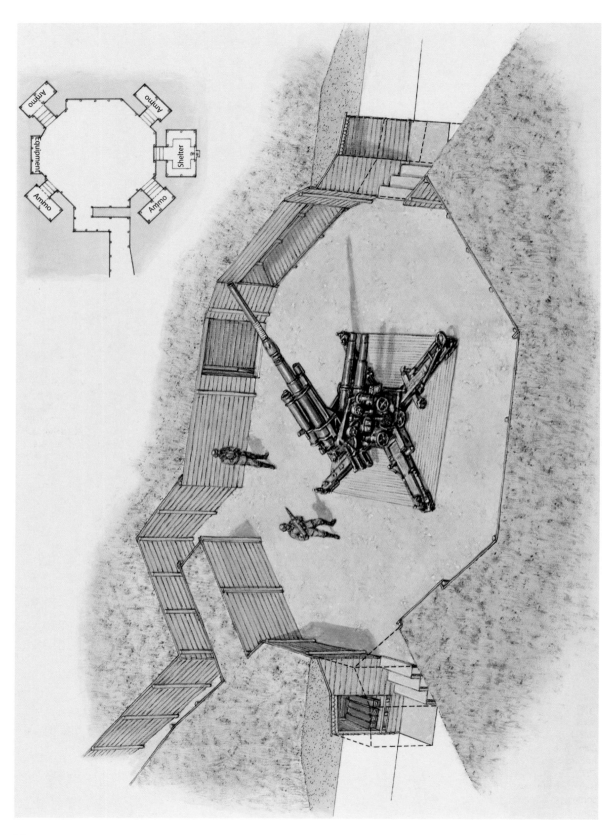

The enhanced emplacement (*erweitere Feldstellung*) was designed to make the position weather-proof and more resistant to battle damage. The floors of the gun-pits were to be covered with concrete, for example, and in general, more concrete or brick was used in construction. This level of protection was also intended to offer better protection against the blast and shrapnel from nearby heavy bombs, although the site itself was not resistant to direct hits. The enhanced emplacement was considered the preferred level of protection for Flak units in homeland defense. In some cases, units that had recently moved would be protected at the lower field standards, but that was only a temporary expedient. The construction of the more elaborate concrete Flak bunkers typical of the Atlantikwall was generally avoided for strategic air defense in Germany for both economic and tactical reasons as mentioned earlier.

The basic element of each battery position was the G-Stand (*Gefechtsstand*, or "battle post") for each Flak gun in the battery. A typical G-Stand had outer walls consisting of an earthen berm with the earth provided by excavating the emplacement to a depth of about a metre (3 feet). When viewed from above, the G-Stand had an octagonal shape with one or two sides serving as entrance to the pit, four sides containing ammunition lockers, one side containing a small emergency shelter for the crew, and another containing a locker for the gun's associated sights and equipment. The small crew shelter within the G-Stand was only intended to provide temporary shelter for the crew when the gun was in operation. Usually, crew quarters were provided in nearby barracks or in an underground shelter (*Unterkunft*). Other major elements of the battery such as the command posts had emplacements similar in construction to the gun-pits. Likewise, searchlight batteries used similar fortification techniques.

Heavy Flak batteries had a large footprint on the ground since the gun pits had to be spaced apart to prevent damage from the gun blast to neighbouring guns and fire-control equipment. The configuration of the heavy Flak battery

TOP LEFT
In 1941–42, the Luftwaffe deployed elevated platforms (*Flakhochstand*) to provide clear fields of fire for light Flak guns in forested regions or in congested areas such as airfields. This shows two of the standard designs, the light 8m (26ft) stand for 20mm guns (left) and the heavy stand 11m (36ft) stand for quadruple 20mm gun, 37mm gun, or the 150cm searchlight (right). The heavy stand here is shown with a special crane fitted that was used to lift the gun into place. A shortage of these in 1944 led many light Flak units in Germany to construct their own out of timber. (NARA)

TOP RIGHT
The Luftwaffe and Kriegsmarine Flak batteries along the Dutch coast were often deployed in L4 and L5 reinforced concrete gun-pits with ammunition lockers protected by steel doors. This is a surviving example in the Hook of Holland area. (Author)

A   REINFORCED 88MM FLAK G-STAND, 1943 PATTERN

This shows the recommended layout for a reinforced gun-pit (*verstärkte Gefechtsstand*) based on the October 1943 Luftwaffe manual, *Flakartillerie: Stellungs- und Befestigungsbau der Flakartillerie: L.Dv.400/11a*. The gun-pit has the standard octagonal shape, with four walls containing munitions lockers, one wall containing an emergency shelter for the crew, and one wall containing a niche for the gun tools and equipment. Reinforced positions such as this would have wood, concrete or gravel for the floor, while the sides would usually be made of timber. The lockers would have a concrete roof for better protection. This gun-pit is 7.5m (25ft) wide and 1.8m (6ft) deep. The next step up in gun-pits was the enhanced field emplacement (*erweitere Feldstellung*) which would substitute more cement and brick instead of wood to make the position more weather-proof.

position evolved during the course of the war, with the arrival of the enlarged batteries. Although the configuration of the gun-pits remained much the same, the layout of the battery's command elements changed once new fire controls, especially radars, became available.

In the early war years from 1939 to 1941, a typical heavy Flak battery was deployed in a circle around its Command Post II (Befehlsstelle II) with the gun-pits about 70–80m (230–62ft) from the centre. Command Post II consisted of a subordinate command section operating a Kommandohilfsgerät 35 (Kdo.Hi.G.35) auxiliary gun director and a small optical range-finder as a back-up for the main gun director. This post also contained electrical junction boxes (*Verteilerkasten*) that fed into the gun pits; one connected to the battery's mobile electrical generators for power, and the other ran to the main command post. The battery's Command Post I (Befehlsstelle I) was usually located at least 100m (328ft) away from the gun-pits to avoid jostling the delicate fire controls by gun blast. The central element of this post was the Kommandogerät 40 gun director (Kdo G. 40), which provided firing data to the guns. The Kommandogerät 40 received early warning data electrically from early-warning radar posts, and had an integral optical range-finder to collect azimuth and angular height data by visual tracking either as the primary source for the guns, or as an adjunct to the radar data in later years as more radars became available. The device produced ballistic solutions and fuze data for the individual guns in the battery and passed this data electrically to the gun pits by cable connections. In contrast to field emplacements, the cabling in static heavy gun batteries was usually buried. One or more generators were positioned near the command post to provide electrical power both to the guns and the command post. In some cases the battery's communications section (*Funkstelle*) was located separately from the command post, but in static positions, it was often located in or near the command post.

The battery command posts increased in complexity as the war went on, and due to the increasing number of expensive electronic devices, the command posts went from simple, cheaply constructed huts to more elaborate shelters of brick or concrete. With the advent of radar, in 1942 the battery command posts began to receive the new Flakumwertegerät Malsi 35. This was a data converter system that would receive target data from the radars, which could then be displayed in the command post on its semi-automated plotting tables. The command post usually received two Malsi tables, and this required the addition of a large room in each command post.

The new *Grossbatterie* tactics introduced in 1942 led to a reconfiguration of Flak batteries, with multiple batteries sharing an amalgamated Flak operations centre instead of individual battery command posts. The old Befehlsstelle II disappeared, and so in the case of a six-gun battery, there would be one gun pit in the centre and the remaining gun pits in a star pattern around it. The fire directors and new fire-control

The change in USAAF tactics after February 1944 saw the growing use of escort fighters to strafe Luftwaffe airfields. To discourage low-altitude attacks, the long-neglected light Flak units of the homeland defense force were shifted to air bases to provide protection. An expedient solution to the strafing attacks was the FlaSL 151 (Fliegerabwehr-Sockellafette mit 3 MG 151), an inexpensive pedestal mount armed with three MG 151 aircraft cannon. This particular example was deployed near an airfield in the Munich area by the 26. Flak-Division in 1945. (MHI)

radars were concentrated at the new operations centre. This new centralized command post would contain one Kdo G. 40 gun director per battery, so there were three at the command post in the case of a three-battery *Grossbatterie*. The most important addition to the command post was a pair of fire direction radars. These were typically the Funkmessgerät. 39 (FuMG. 39) or FuMG. 41. One fire control radar was used to control the gun-directors and to maintain track of the targeted enemy bomber formation, while the other radar was kept free to search for other formations, or to conduct supplementary scans of the targeted formation to select the most lucrative targets.

The new operations centre shelter continued to expand due to the sophistication of the data flowing into it from the early-warning network and the increasing number of communication devices and plotting displays. By 1943, the typical operations centre had a switchboard room for communications, a cable room for junctions for its own sensors and remote data sources, a map room, a data room for remote data panels and a plotting room containing two Malsi 35 plotting tables. The Malsi plotting tables took on a new importance after the RAF introduced radar jamming tactics such as Window in the summer of 1943. The Malsi could accept data from neighbouring batteries, neighbouring radars, or the command post's own optical directors, so that in the event of Allied radar jamming, the Grossbatterie could still engage its targets.

Light Flak revival

Although the Flak divisions continued to deploy light Flak batteries through the war years, they had little value in homeland defense due to the high operating altitudes of British and American bombers. This began to change after January 1944 when the US Eighth Air Force launched more aggressive fighter tactics and began to encourage low-altitude sweeps against German airfields. Suddenly, there was an immediate need for light Flak. The situation grew progressively worse through 1944 as the Allied armies advanced into Germany and the number of Allied fighter planes roaming in German air space increased. The focus of early USAAF fighter attacks in early 1944 were German airfields as part of Operation *Pointblank,* the mission to smash the German fighter force prior to the D-Day landings. As a result, the Luftwaffe began to transfer idle light Flak units to participate in airfield defense. This is very evident on the map of the Munich area shown on page 15 where most of the light Flak sections are deployed near airfields or communication hubs. Light Flak units used static emplacements essentially similar to the heavy Flak batteries, except that the fire control posts tended to be less elaborate since heavy Flak had priority for radar.

The increasing number of light Flak batteries positioned around German airfield in early 1944 led to evolving USAAF fighter tactics, especially the use of low-level manoeuvres to minimize exposure to light Flak. These low-level tactics encouraged the Luftwaffe light Flak units to deploy some of their batteries on elevated Flak stands (*Flakhochstanden*) which provided better fields of fire, especially in situations where there were obstacles such as buildings or wooded areas. The Luftwaffe had already developed a family of prefabricated modular steel platforms early in the war. There were two light Flak stands for the 20mm guns in 5m (15ft) and 8m (28ft) configurations, as well as a heavy Flak stand 11m (36ft) high which could be used for the quadruple 20mm gun, 37mm gun, or the 150cm searchlight. Although these could be disassembled and moved, sudden demand in mid-

1944 meant that they were in short supply. As a result, many light Flak batteries began constructing wooden platforms patterned on the steel version using available resources. Alternately, light Flak guns were placed on the roofs of high buildings.

Atlantikwall Flak

The steady drone of RAF aircraft along the "bomber Autobahn" over the Netherlands and into Germany encouraged the Luftwaffe to create its densest air defense zone in this sector. Kammhuber's main command post, for example, was located at Zeist in the Netherlands. However, the Luftwaffe's night-fighter force did not want to become entangled with the dense concentrations of Flak batteries for fear of "friendly fire" incidents, so this area did not receive high priority for Luftwaffe heavy Flak batteries in 1940–43. Nevertheless, the opportunity to take shots at British bombers both as they approached and departed Germany was too good to ignore. In 1942, a Flak belt was established in the Low Countries along the north coast where it was too far forward to interfere with the Kammhuber Line. This had been a traditional role for the Kriegsmarine during World War I, when a naval Flak group had been deployed with the Marinekorps Flandern along the North Sea coast. The new program became wrapped up in the Atlantikwall effort, since the Marineflak could serve a dual role in anti-invasion defense against surface targets, as well as in air defense against the RAF. Eventually some 23 Marineflak heavy batteries were deployed in the Netherlands, from the Hook of Holland to the German coast.[2]

Since these Marineflak batteries were positioned along the coast, they were deployed in heavily fortified bunkers like other elements of the Atlantikwall. These fortified positions were laid out much the same as Luftwaffe heavy Flak batteries, but the emplacements were constructed of steel-reinforced concrete instead of earth berms and timber. The associated crew and ammunition shelters were fully protected bunkers, able to withstand direct bomb hits or naval shelling. Two of the more common gun bunkers used by the Marineflak in the Netherlands were the Fl.243 Schwere Flakstand and the later Luftwaffe L 401 Geschützstand für 8,8 oder 10,5cm Flak. These

---

[2] For further details of these Marineflak batteries see: Steven Zaloga, *The Atlantic Wall (2): Belgium, the Netherlands, Denmark, and Norway* (Osprey Fortress 89, 2009).

B   WASSERFALL FLAK MISSILE BATTERY SITE, PROPOSAL B

The shape of things to come. The declining effectiveness of conventional Flak led the Luftwaffe to design first-generation Flak missiles, of which the Wasserfall C2 ("waterfall") was the most advanced. The first two batteries were expected to be operational in late 1945, with about 300 more by the end of 1946. In April 1943, three configurations of battery emplacement were proposed: from a simple site with unprotected hangers (*Entwurf* A ["Proposal A"]), a partially fortified site as seen here (*Entwurf* B) and a fully fortified site with the missile stored in a single bunker (*Entwurf* C). The intention was to store 80 missiles per battery site, with a total of eight launch pads, and the capability to fire about 35 missiles against a single bomber formation. The Entwurf B Batteriestellung shown here had two octagonal concrete launch bunkers, each containing 16 missiles on their wheeled launch pads; each of the eight launch cells would wheel out one missile at a time, while the second missile in each cell was being prepared for the next launch sequence. The early versions of the missile employed the Burgund command-guidance system, but the ultimate fire-control shown here is the radar command-guided Rheinland A system. The Mannheim-Rüse radar served as the battery's search and track system. The two bunkers were each fitted with a Rheingold fire-control radar working in conjunction with a Kehlheim command station (not visible here). Besides the two launch bunkers, the battery site also had a command post with an attached maintenance/preparation hangar. Although Wasserfall never entered production, it was a stepping stone to the first Soviet surface-to-air missile (SAM) in 1950, the S-25 Berkut (NATO: SA-1 Guild).

had the gun-pit located on the top of the bunker, and a fully protected shelter for the crew underneath. Some batteries had their guns in a simple concrete kettle gun-pit, such as the L4 and L5 designs, with the crew shelter located separately. A portion of the Marineflak batteries had their guns protected in fully-armored steel turrets. The heavy Marineflak batteries in the Netherlands were most often equipped with the Rheinmetall-Borsig 105mm SK C/32.

The Luftwaffe had an extensive presence in the Atlantikwall program, primarily involved in the deployment of an array of early warning posts. These included numerous long-range early radars including Mammut and Freya radars, as well as other types of early warning sensors and electronic signals interception posts that were used to alert Luftwaffe fighter and Flak units in Germany of impending RAF and USAAF bomber raids. As in the case of the Marineflak, the proximity of these sites to the coast led to the decision that they would be fortified with bunker-type crew shelters.

Germany's heavy investment in Flak artillery failed to defeat Allied heavy bombers. The Flak force consumed between a quarter and a third of Wehrmacht ordnance and ammunition production; the associated radars and communications equipment consumed half the military electronics production. The failure was not so much the Flak guns, which were the best in the world, but the leadership in the senior ranks of the Luftwaffe who failed to appreciate the central importance of modern electronics to air defense. Germany was slow to field an integrated air defense network, and failed to keep pace with Britain in electronic warfare. The Flak batteries became increasingly blind after the summer of 1943 as the RAF employed ever more sophisticated electronic warfare tactics. The USAAF added to the problem, backed as it was by America's prodigious electronics industry, which flooded the skies with new radars, jammers and other electronic warfare aids. Flak might have been partly redeemed by the introduction of a radio-frequency proximity fuze like the American VT fuze, but once again, poor allotment of resources in 1942–43 delayed the development of this critical technology. Germany turned instead to even more exotic weapons, such as radar-guided anti-aircraft missiles, but this was another case of overly ambitious schemes started much too late. The arguments about the effectiveness of Flak in 1940–45 are too complex to cover in detail in this short book.

AIR-RAID FORTIFICATIONS

Pre-war initiatives

There was a great uneasiness about the threat of bomber attack throughout most of Europe in the 1930s. Germany had attacked British cities during World War I using Zeppelins and bombers, and there was a widespread presumption that bomber attack against cities and factories would become a feature of future wars. There was particular concern that bomber attacks would include the use of chemical weapons. Popular novels and science fiction of the day depicted the apocalyptic horrors of gas attack against unprotected cities. The dilemma facing Germany was the extent of air defense needed both for active air defenses, such as fighter aircraft and anti-aircraft guns, as well as passive defenses, such as air-raid shelters for civilians and military personnel. Hitler and the Nazi Party were inclined towards offensive use of air power, which would presumably avoid the need for extensive and expensive air defense preparations, and so Germany's early work in this field was less comprehensive than in Britain.

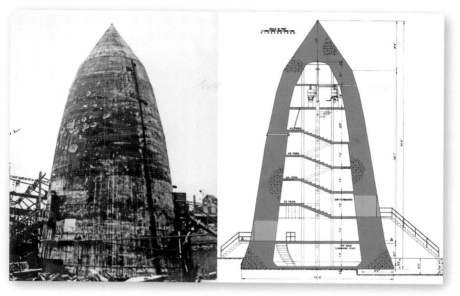

A battle-scarred Winkel tower in the ruins of the Gelsenkirchener Benzin synthetic fuel plant in Buer-Scholven. This particular plant was hit by 246 tons of bombs in the USAAF raid on October 30, 1944, and this air-raid shelter was one of the few structures to survive. To the right is a scale cross-section of the Typ 1c tower showing the internal layout and prepared by a post-war US bombing survey team. (NARA)

During the 1920s, the German government took its first tentative steps towards organizing air-raid-protection services, mainly managed by the Ministry of the Interior through the police. Popular organizations such as the Deutsche Luftschutz-Liga (German Air Defense League) attempted to drum up popular support for a more vigorous defense effort. These early endeavours were intended to inform the general public about the air threat, to formulate plans for the construction of air-raid shelters and the manufacture of gas-masks, and to encourage voluntary public participation in air defense.

It was only after Hitler's accession to power in 1933 that plans became more formal. In June 1933, the shadow Luftwaffe under Hermann Göring announced the formation of National Air Raid Protection League (*Reichsluftschutzbund*, or RLB). The RLB was organized on a regional basis

The Winkel towers proved very effective during the war. These two Typ 1c Winkel towers were located in the Focke-Wulf Werke plant in Bremen and as can be seen, the rest of the factory was completely devastated by Allied bombing raids but the towers remained largely intact. (NARA)

by province (*Landes*), regions (*Gaue*), area (*Kreis*), and district (*Orts*) down through local leaders at block and building level. Overall military supervision of the air-raid protection effort was undertaken by a special inspectorate of the Führungsstab 1A of the Luftwaffe's general staff, first located in Wannsee near Berlin, and later in Tangermunde. The air-raid protection law signed by Hitler in August 1935 made it a duty of all German citizens to participate in this program, and established the practice that there would be no government compensation for personal service. The government in Berlin gradually absorbed more control over the process, with Heinrich Himmler taking control of police work in air-raid protection after the summer of 1936 through the interior ministry. The first major decree on air-raid protection was released in May 1937 and broadly outlined the structure that would be in place throughout the war.

The 1937 decree formed the basis for subsequent air-raid-shelter policy. A Reichsgruppe Industrie was established to supervise the new *Werkluftschutz* ("industrial air-raid protection service") and to encourage the construction of large shelters adjacent to factories and major commercial enterprises. The *Erweiterselbschutz* ("extended self-protection service") was intended to manage air-raid protection for public and private buildings, as well as smaller commercial and industrial buildings. Air-raid-protection for homes and smaller private and public buildings was subordinated to the new *Selbschutz* ("self-defense service"), which encouraged the construction of private shelters and managed the air-raid warden system. The RLB was nominally a voluntary organization, but was in fact directed by the Nazi Party to encourage public participation in air-raid efforts. It eventually had a membership of 13 million and dues were used to inform and educate the general public about air-raid protection, as well as to provide minor items such as gas-masks to civilians too poor to purchase them. In general, the RLB's function was primarily supervisory and educational, while the actual management of air-raid protection was overseen by the local police and fire services.

The *Werkluftschutz* industrial defense service initiated the first round of shelter construction in the late 1930s, especially for those areas deemed most vulnerable to air attack. This included major military plants, as well as other likely targets such as railway centres. Some sites that were exceptionally vulnerable to bomber attack, such as the naval base at Wilhelmshaven on the North Sea, saw the creation of bomb-proof shelters sooner than most other areas. Likewise, the Kriegsmarine began shelter construction at its most vulnerable ports such as Wilhelmshaven. However, large-scale construction of public air-raid shelters did not begin until after the start of the war.

Until the late 1930s, there were few systematic studies of modern air-raid shelters. The Institute for Air Defense Construction (IfBL, or Institut für Baulichen Luftschutz) was created under Prof. Dr. Theodor Kristen at the Technischen Hochschule Braunschweig to establish national standards for the construction of public air-raid shelters. Many of the early industrial shelters were designed by private engineering firms. The initial designs also addressed the need for gas protection, and a number of industrial firms began mass-production of gas-proof doors, filtration systems, and other components that could be incorporated into bomb shelters.

The shock of the RAF raids on Berlin in August and September 1940 forced Hitler to initiate the Führer-Sofortprogramm ("emergency program") on 10 October 1940 to protect Germany's urban population with public air-raid shelters. The original scheme was to create about 6,000 bomb-proof bunkers, as well as many "splinter-proof" shelters for 35 million civilians in 92 cities. The original scheme would have required the fantastic total of 200 million cubic metres (260 million cubic yards) of concrete, about as much as the past two decades of civil construction. To put this in perspective, the Maginot Line had consumed 1.5 million cubic metres (2 million cubic yards) of concrete and the Atlantikwall program in France in 1942–44 used 17 million cubic metres (22 million cubic yards). Needless to say, these overly ambitious goals did not come close to realization.

The early LS-Hochbunker had extensive fittings to make prolonged stays in the shelters as comfortable as possible. This is a view inside the Kaiserstrasse air-raid bunker in Krefeld and shows the typical configuration early in the war with wooden bunk beds. Once the shelters became overcrowded in 1944–45, the bunk-beds were removed to permit more people to take shelter in the bunkers. (NARA)

Due to the enormity of the work, the program was undertaken in three phases, with various cities categorized by priority (*Luftschutz-Orten.1, .2, .3*). The 70 highest priority cities were assigned to Phase 1 (*Welle.1*) with construction starting in November 1940 and the completion planned for November 1941. The program was managed by the Luftwaffe's Inspektion.13 (L.In.13) led by Dr. Kurt Knipfer, and the construction was overseen by the Organization Todt (OT) paramilitary construction administration. Unlike military projects such as the Westwall or the later Atlantikwall, the Sofortprogramm was decentralized and there was less standardization of designs. Berlin delegated responsibility for much of the effort to local municipal governments and industry. The initial wave of the Sofortprogramm was intended to provide bomb-proof bunker shelters

This LS-Hockbunker was designed by the architect Hans Schuhmacher and located on Kluckstrasse in Cologne. It has Schuhmacher's distinctive "church bunker" style akin to those on Helenenwallstrasse and Marktstrasse. This particular bunker was hit with a large bomb that blew away about half of the ornamental roof. The roof acted as a burster slab, detonating the bomb before it hit the main roof. The bunker's main horizontal roof was 1.4m (4.7ft) of steel-reinforced concrete. (NARA)

for about 5 percent of the population in the key cities, while the remainder of the population would have to make do with less robust *Splittersichere* ("splinter-proof") shelters, which were primarily expedient adaptations of existing buildings and tunnels.

Basement shelters

By far the most common form of public shelter was the reinforced basement. These were classified at the lower "splinter-proof" standard since they could not withstand a direct bomb hit. In general, *Luftschutz Kellar* ("basement air-raid shelters") were limited to a capacity of 50 to 100 persons. Most large apartment buildings had shelters created in their cellars. Where possible, the basements were upgraded with gas protection by sealing windows, adding an

Another good example of an early LS-Hochbunker with extensive architectural detail including an ornamental roof and gables. Located on Sandweg in the Rochuspark suburbs of Cologne, it was designed by the architect Ernst Nolte and was completed in 1942. Local inhabitants used it as a refuge during the fighting on the western banks of the Rhine in March 1945, and some of the occupants have come out to wave a white flag during the approach of tanks of the 3rd Armored Division on March 5, 1945. After the war, it was converted into flats. (NARA)

intermediate gas-lock room (*Gasschleuse*) at the main entrance, and incorporating a gas filter. Gas locks were small anterooms located in front of the main entrance door. They were intended to provide a space where civilians contaminated by chemical agents could be scrubbed clean before entering the shelter. The shelter entrance itself was protected by a gas-proof door.

Air-raid basements were reinforced with wood or steel beams to minimize the risk that they would be crushed if the building above collapsed during a bombing attack. German cities had a well-established construction practice of erecting fire-walls between buildings to prevent the spread of fire between buildings that shared common walls, but these walls could inadvertently trap

LS-Hochbunker design became increasingly frugal and simplified as the supply of concrete and labour became scarce. This LS-Hochbunker in Krefeld in March 1945 has a false roof to help it blend in better with the surrounding neighbourhood, but it is otherwise unadorned. (NARA)

civilians in the basement shelters. As a result, a program began to create passageways between buildings by cutting through the walls, and creating a more modest fire barrier with thinner brick that could be readily demolished if necessary for escape. Public shelters were very clearly marked by signs, and large white arrows were painted on walls near the entrance as an aid at night-time due to the black-out measures.

Enclosed trench shelters

In general, new underground shelters were not the favoured design solution in Germany during the Sofortprogramm. However, in some places, such as factories where basements were not present, simple underground structures at shallow depths provided a quick and easy means to rapidly create air-raid shelters. These were called *Deckungsgräben* ("enclosed trenches"), or sometimes *Splittersicheregräben* ("splinter-protected trenches"). Variations on this design

This LS-Hochbunker in Krefeld in March 1945 is typical of bunkers built in 1943 in a simple style with little or no architectural detail. It had a capacity of about 10,000 people. The structure on the roof is part of the ventilation system. There were 11 large air-raid bunkers in the Krefeld area during the war. (NARA)

using circular concrete castings were called *Röhrenbunker* ("tube bunkers"). The enclosed trenches were strongly influenced by World War I trench fortification techniques. The crudest versions were simply trenches lined with wood, with a plank roof covered by a few feet of earth, although efforts were made to create more permanent and durable structures. By 1940, a number of German firms were offering prefabricated steel sections that could be used to create a metal-lined enclosed trench. However, industrial priorities for weapons production soon reduced the availability of steel for such projects. Organization Todt encouraged the use of prefabricated concrete sections, both for oval and rectangular structures. In addition, other forms of normal construction material such as brick and concrete block were widely used.

The enclosed trench shelters were generally designed to accommodate 100 to 500 persons, although the Organization Todt instruction book offered five standard designs for 15, 50, 100, 150 and 200 persons. The most common size was for 50 persons, and larger shelters were usually created by combining several 50-person sections. The standard practice was to avoid a single long tube, and either to stagger the sections with a slight off-set at the joint, or configure the sections in a zig-zag fashion or at right angles to one another. This was a standard tactic of World War I trench design and was intended to prevent the entire structure being destroyed if only one section was penetrated by a bomb.

Enclosed trench shelters were supposed to be completely buried for the best protection, but some were constructed in a partially submerged configuration, and others were built entirely on the surface with earth packed around them. These enclosed trench shelters were the second most common form of air-raid shelter in Germany during the war in terms of overall numbers. For example, the city of Osnabruck had about 650 air-raid shelters of which about 200 were concrete-enclosed trenches. Of these, about 90 were public shelters capable of accommodating about 13,000 people, while the remaining 110 were smaller privately built structures capable of housing about 2,150 people. The construction of enclosed trench shelters continued throughout the war since they required modest resources. Indeed, by 1944 when the construction of the large air-raid bunkers generally stopped due to the lack of material, enclosed-trench construction continued as an inexpensive, albeit less effective, alternative.

Air defense bunkers

The primary type of bomb-proof shelter under the 1940 Sofortprogramm was the *Luftschutz-Bunker* (LS-Bunker). They were also called *Hochbunker* ("high bunker") to distinguish them from the underground types. The intention of the 1940 Sofortprogramm was to provide bunker protection for about 5 percent of the city population, usually those in critical government and industrial positions and near government and industrial facilities. Pre-war studies of shelter design examined both underground and surface shelters and concluded that surface shelters were more economical to build than underground designs. The Brunswick IfBL also studied the relationship of bunker size and cost, and concluded that larger shelters were more economical. For example, a typical LS-Bunker design for 500 persons required 3 cubic metres (4 cubic yards) of concrete per person, while a design for 4,000 persons required only 1.8 cubic metres (3 cubic yards). The LS-Bunker program was controversial and it was opposed by some senior Luftwaffe technical officers who argued that it would be better to spread out the limited construction resources to give all civilians a certain level of protection rather than concentrating it on only a small number of places. Generalmajor W. Lindner, head of the technical division of the Luftwaffe's civil defense effort, argued that the LS-Bunker program was "a bad policy psychologically because it tended to concentrate people in distant shelters, when it would have been more convenient to be sheltered near their homes and therefore available to defend them against incendiary attacks." He favoured both improved cellar shelters and more enclosed trenches.

The earliest forms of LS-Bunker was the air-raid tower (*Luftschutz-Türm*, or LS-Türm) which first began to appear in the mid-1930s. They were primarily intended for industrial sites, and the main attraction of this configuration was that it did not take up a great deal of acreage on a site. It was especially suitable for existing rail yards, dockyards, and factories where space was already at a premium. The conical cap of the tower was designed to deflect any bomb impacts, with the presumption that the bomb would skid off the steep roof and fall to the base of the tower which was much thicker and better prepared to absorb the bomb's explosion. The most common of these was the LS-Türm der Bauart Winkel developed by the Leo Winkel firm in Duisburg from 1934. The Winkel towers were distinctive for their futuristic bullet shape; in Germany they were named *Zuckerhut* ("sugar loaf") after a popular cone-shaped holiday

By 1945, life in the wartime public air-raid bunkers was cramped and uncomfortable, but it was infinitely safer than most other alternatives. This is the interior of the shelter in Krefeld shown in the accompanying photo. By this stage, the city had been captured by the Ninth US Army and so no longer had to fear bomber attacks. However, many civilians remained in the shelters since their homes had been destroyed, and others used the shelters to avoid artillery shelling by the Wehrmacht. (NARA)

confection. A prototype Winkel tower was tested at the Luftwaffe's Rechlin proving ground and was subsequently adopted by the railway repair yards of the Reichsbahn. About 200 Winkel towers were built in several different models, constituting about a third of all of the towers built during the war. Other architectural firms favoured a neo-Romantic style hinting at medieval castle towers and using different internal layouts as shown in the accompanying plate on page 50. Often, a firm's design won regional appeal, so for example, the LS-Türm der Bauart Zombeck developed by the Paul Zombeck firm in Dortmund in 1937 was adopted in Hamburg and 12 were built there, primarily near the main city railway stations. The typical LS-Türm could accommodate 500 people, but some of the larger designs could accommodate over a thousand and even more under emergency circumstances. Large-scale construction of the LS-Türm began in 1940 and about 500–600 were built. The towers were not as efficient in terms of material as more conventional "blockhouse" styles, and the

construction of some designs became less common after national construction standards were released in the summer of 1941 that specified the ratio of concrete per occupant.

Although the tower bunkers were the earliest and most distinctive air-raid bunkers, more conventional rectangular blockhouse designs predominated in urban areas during the war years. The rectangular bunkers were simpler and less expensive to build. The basic requirement in 1940 was for roof protection of at least 1.4m (4.5ft) of steel-reinforced concrete for the roof and at least 1.1m (3.5ft) for the side-walls, which was believed to be adequate

ABOVE
Although many shelter bunkers were built away from other structures, some were integrated into existing neighbourhoods such as this LS-Hochbunker at Kornerstrasse 107–111 in Cologne. It was designed by the architect Hans Schuhmacher and built in 1942–43 with accommodation for 1,550 people and 1,700 square metres (18,000 square feet) of floor space. It still exists today. (NARA)

LEFT
This is another example of a LS-Hochbunker constructed within an existing neighbourhood of flats on Herthastrasse in Cologne. It was designed by the architect Ernst Nolte and built in 1942 with accommodation for 2,700 people and 2,715 square metres (29,000 square feet) of floor space. As can be seen, the bunker survived the bombing raids but the neighbouring apartment buildings have been gutted. This bunker still remains in Cologne, though has been heavily rebuilt. (NARA)

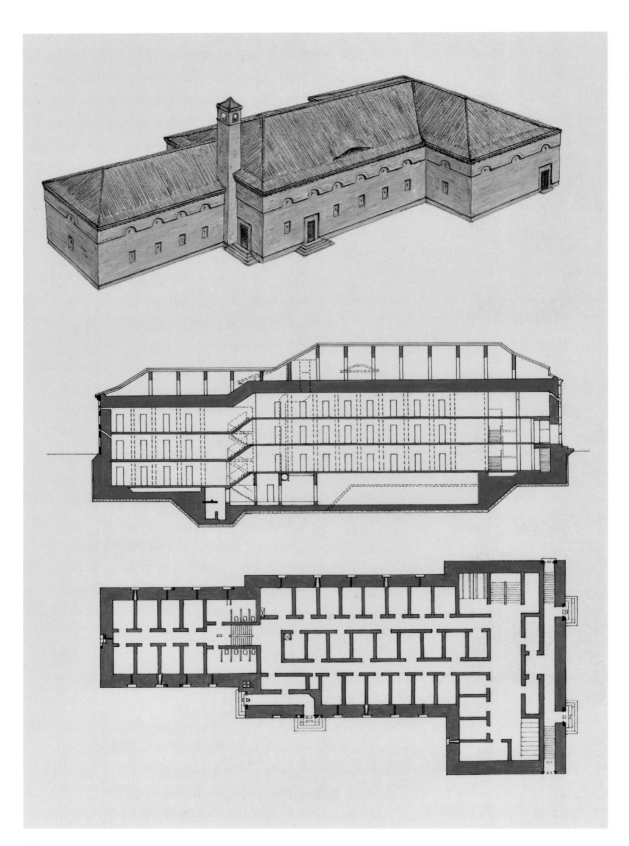

Although the bunkers offered excellent protection, they were by no means invulnerable. The air-raid bunkers suffered at least 120 direct hits during the course of the war, with known casualties of about 500. This two-story LS-Hochbunker on Rupprechtstrasse in Cologne was hit directly on the roof slab by a 900–1,800kg (2,000–4,000lb) bomb which penetrated the interior. This particular facility was designed by the architect Helmuth Wirminghaus with a capacity for 1,825 people and floor space of 1,070 square metres (11,500 square feet); it still exists today and has been used for office and factory space. (NARA)

This view shows an LS-Hochbunker built on Kornerstrasse in Hagen in 1941 intended to protect against 250kg (500lb) bombs. Although designed to accommodate 600 people, on the night of March 15, 1945, there were about 6,000 civilians in the structure when it was struck on the side by a heavy bomb in the 900–1,800kg range (2,000–4,000lb), killing about 290 people. (NARA)

C   LS-HOCHBUNKER, TACITUSSTRASSE, COLOGNE

This was a fairly typical example of the 1940–41 period urban air-raid shelters, designed to better blend into their local surroundings with false roofs and architectural adornment. This bunker resembles the several other *Kirchenbunker* ("church bunkers") designed by Hans Schuhmacher in Cologne, with their distinctive steeples. This three-story bunker was designed to accommodate 1,490 people and had 1,560 square metres of floor space (16,800 square feet). In 1942–43, the building was used by the Nazi party's regional administration (NSDAP-Gauleitung) and after the war, it was used by the Bundeswehr.

The effectiveness of the LS-Bunker concept is nowhere more evident than this aerial photo of a LS-Hochbunker in Bremen in 1945 with all the neighbouring homes completely burned out and gutted while the shelter remains intact and undamaged. (NARA)

against the 250kg (500lb) bombs common at the time. Since steel was at a premium, a variety of concrete reinforcement techniques were used. The traditional "cubical" method used steel reinforcing bars (rebar) uniformly distributed through the concrete casting. This method was standard in German bunker construction such as the Westwall, but this soon proved to be too expensive for the poorly funded shelter effort. In late 1940, a new technique was adopted in some bunkers, using spiral steel mats which reduced the amount of steel used for reinforcement, but which was somewhat complex to construct. Eventually, both approaches were replaced by the Brunswick style of reinforcement developed by the IfBL, which reduced the steel rebar near the surface, but concentrated it near the inner face of the slab. This reduced steel use from 300kg per cubic metre in the traditional cubical method to only 30kg (66lb). By 1941, Kristen's IfBL recommended that the minimum standard for the bunkers be increased to 2.5m (8ft) to deal with the threat of 1,000kg (2,000lb) bombs. The Luftwaffe refused and set the minimum instead as 2m (6.5ft), though many cities adopted the 2.5m (8ft) standard based on Kristen's recommendations.

In July 1941, the Luftwaffe released a set of pamphlets on air defense shelters that laid out basic design requirements. Three basic construction levels (*Baustufe*) of bunkers varied by the thickness of the roofs and walls: Baustufe A (3m/10ft); Baustufe B (2.5m/8ft) and Baustufe C (2m/6.5ft). The recommended designs were also tailored to the size of the building with the higher A level of protection being intended for large shelters of 1,500–3,000 people, B standards for 300–1,500, and C standards for small bunkers under 300 people. The 1941 instructions provided only a basic guideline for the design of the bunkers, and these were usually developed in more detail by local architectural firms. Some cities adopted their own common designs. Hanover, for example, adopted five standard designs designated as B, C, H.I, H.II, and H.III, with several intermediate variations; the H.II.4 bunker used the basic H.II floor-plan, but had four floors, for example.

The early bunkers offered a relatively high level of comfort to their inhabitants. They were provided with bunk beds, toilet, and wash facilities, an independent electrical supply for lighting and air filtration, and a heating system for the winter months. The early designs also went to some lengths to blend into the local neighbourhoods. This was done in part to satisfy urban planners, who abhorred the military's ugly concrete bunker designs, but a secondary reason was for camouflage.

Although the 1940 Sofortprogramm did not favour the construction of large underground air-raid bunkers (LS-Tiefbunker), a number of these were built during the war. Due to their high cost, they were constructed mainly at political and military headquarters. The best known of the deep bunkers was the Führerbunker, constructed in the Chancellery building (Reichskanzlei) in Berlin. The original bunker was built under the garden of the Chancellery from 1936. When the new Chancellery was built, portions of the basement were earmarked for use as air-raid shelters. With the intensification of RAF bombing of Berlin in 1943, a deeper bunker was added, with the old bunker being renamed as the Vorbunker and the new bunker becoming the well-known Führerbunker where Hitler spent his final days. Aside from the Führerbunker, the most notorious of the deep bunkers was the LS-Tiefbunker built near the harbour in Danzig near the contemporary Plac Dominikanski. In 1945 during the siege of Festung Danzig, Red Army artillery knocked out the pumps used to drain the water out of the bunker, and rubble blocked the exits. As many as 4,500 people inside were drowned in what was probably the single worst air-raid shelter calamity of the war.

Tunnels were sometimes used for air-raid shelters and known as LS-Tiefstollen. In some cases they were expressly built for this function, but the majority of air-raid tunnels were existing railroad and mining tunnels adapted to this function and were not purpose-built. The mixture of bomb-proof shelters varied by region, but in the case of the heavily bombed north Rhine region, 76.5 percent were surface bunkers, 11.8 percent were underground bunkers and 11.7 percent were tunnel shelters.

Besides normal air-raid shelters, many cities installed specialized hospital bunkers (*Krankenhausbunker*). This particular example was one of the largest air-raid bunkers in southern Germany and was located in Frankfurt-am-Main. (NARA)

No doubt the most famous air-raid bunker in Berlin was the Führerbunker located under the Chancellery building. Here, British foreign secretary Ernest Bevin is given a tour of the area near the bunker entrance on August 2, 1945 during the "Big Three" conference. Hitler's body was discovered by the Red Army a short distance from this entrance. (NARA)

Military shelters

Besides the civilian air-raid shelters, a variety of military air-raid shelters were constructed in parallel to the Sofortprogramm. The Kriegsmarine was the most active service in Germany in 1940–41 since the naval bases such as Wilhelmshaven and Bremen were so vulnerable to RAF bomber attack. The Kriegsmarine developed a number of standard air-raid bunkers (*Truppenmannschafsbunkeren*). The T-750, with a capacity for 750 troops, was one of the best-known types in the port cities.

The Luftwaffe did not fortify its airbases as heavily in Germany as it did in occupied Europe. Luftwaffe airbases in France, the Low Countries, and Scandinavia often had numerous small bunkers and pillboxes to serve as defenses against paratroop attack. This was a less serious threat in Germany itself, with correspondingly fewer strongpoints. Some airfields in Germany had reinforced command post bunkers (*Gefechtsstand*) but in general, the accent was on functional architecture rather than defensive works. When the threat of Allied fighter strafing increased in 1944, there was some effort to reinforce airfields in Germany, including an extensive effort to erect protective berms (*Splitterboxen*) around aircraft parking spaces; hardened aircraft shelters were not especially common. The Luftwaffe also had an extensive network of air defense command posts, often contained in large reinforced bunkers.

The Flak towers

As mentioned earlier, Hitler was so enraged by the first RAF raids against Berlin that he ordered the construction of massive Flak towers in Berlin based on his own sketches. This program started in September 1940 and pre-dated the Sofortprogramm by a month. Although called Flak towers (*Flaktürme*) they were actually large air-raid shelters with Flak batteries on top. Hitler envisioned the towers as a means to remind the citizenry of Germany's defiance of the British bombers, but also as a means to shelter precious museum artefacts and public documents. Any surplus space could be used for public air-raid shelters.

The sheer size of the proposed structures presented daunting design problems. Although the construction of the first Berlin towers was nominally under the control of Hitler's personal architect, Albert Speer, the design work was actually undertaken by one of his subordinates, Prof. Friedrich Tamms. He completed preliminary designs and models in October 1940 with detailed drawings finished in March 1941 for Hitler's approval. The Flak towers came in two varieties, the basic *Gefechtstürm* (G-Türm) mounting the Flak battery, and a supporting *Leittürm* (L-Türm) with an associated fire-control radar. The initial plan was for six pairs in Berlin, but spacing issues between the towers eventually limited the Berlin deployment to three pairs. For a time, there were plans to convert the Reichstag building into a Flak tower, but this scheme was eventually abandoned.

The principal armament of the Flak towers was intended to be four sets of twin 128mm anti-aircraft guns. However, the first towers were armed with four single 105mm Flak guns, replaced by the 128mm Flakzwilling 40 guns once they entered serial production in September 1942. The supplementary batteries were armed with 20mm and 37mm automatic cannon.

Once the "Zoo-Bunker" was completed, work began on two more Flak complexes in Berlin, the Gefechtstürm II in the Friedrichshain district, completed in October 1941 and the Gefechtstürm III in the Humboldthain district completed in April 1942. As in the case of the Tiergarten towers, Gefechtstürm II was used to house the treasures of the Kaiser Wilhelm museum. The fourth complex was built in Hamburg in the Heiligeistfeld area and was built on the same pattern as the Berlin towers.

During the course of construction of the first Flak complexes, Tamm's team had developed a simplified and smaller tower for future construction, variously called Typ 2 or Bauart 2, which was used for the first time with Gefechtstürm VI located in the Wilhelmsburg district of Hamburg, completed in October 1942. This was the second and last complex built in

The fourth of the Flak towers to be completed was the "Holy Ghost bunker," Gefechtstürm IV in the Heiligengeistfeld area in Hamburg. It was built on the same Typ 1 pattern as the Berlin towers and was completed in October 1942. (NARA)

Hamburg. In the meantime, Hitler had ordered the construction of Flak towers in Vienna, and the Gefechtstürm VIII in the Arenberg Park used the Typ 2 configuration when it was completed in October 1943.

The last two towers built in Vienna were the final Typ 3 configuration, which had a markedly different design than the previous types, with a circular base for the Gefechtstürm compared to the rectangular base in the previous two designs. The first of these, the Gefechtstürm V was completed in the courtyard of the Stiftskaserne in Vienna in September 1943, with the associated Leittürm V located in nearby Esterházy Park. The final tower was also in the Typ 3 configuration and Gefechtstürm VII was built in the Augarten district of Vienna in 1944.

The "sparrow's nests" on the sides of the Flak towers were used for light Flak positions such as this 37mm gun on Gefechtstürm IV in Hamburg. As can be seen, this particular position took a bomb hit during the war. (NARA)

One-man bunkers

At the opposite end of the size spectrum from the massive Flak towers were the ubiquitous *Brandwachenständ* (BWS, or "fire warden stand"). They were also called *Splitterschutzzellen* (SSZ, or "splinter-proof compartment") or *Einmannbunker* ("one-man bunker"). These were developed by private firms in the early 1930s for security guards at factories. The early designs were most often constructed from steel, and so provided ballistic protection. They began to attract government attention during the early war years due to their obvious utility for a variety of military and civil defense applications. The most common air defense application was as a shelter for fire wardens. German air defense practice assigned fire wardens the task of directing stray

A view of the Hamburg Gefechtstürm IV in the Heiligengeistfeld district. After the war, it was turned into emergency apartments for war refugees, and in 1956 was converted into the Hochhaus II art centre. (NARA)

civilians to air-raid shelters during an air-raid. In addition, the fire departments needed observers around the city to provide information on fires or other problems. The BWS provided a means of security for the fire warden in the midst of an air-raid.

Although the early BWS were often of steel construction, during the war years, they were increasingly made from concrete. The concrete offered better insulation than steel, and was more widely available after 1941 when steel was reserved for military needs. Thousands of these small shelters were built during the war by numerous small private firms. Although used mainly for fire wardens, they continued to be used for other security applications by industrial guards, railroad guards, concentration camps, and military police. They became ubiquitous through occupied Europe, and were often erected as guard posts near German bases and military facilities. When the Allied armies reached German soil in 1944–45, these small positions were often used as improvised tactical defense points. Besides the small cupola-style BWS, a large variety of other fire warden structures were built during the war. Reinforced concrete towers were also used in some areas to provide the fire wardens with greater visibility of the surrounding area.

The bombing intensifies

The Sofortprogramm was delayed by the invasion of Russia in June 1941, which drained the country of military trucks and also led to the dispatch of most army and navy construction battalions to new assignments. Although the plan had been to complete Phase I by November 1941, this was delayed until the spring of 1942 in many locations. By the beginning of 1942, 1,215 bunkers had been completed and 515 more were under construction by year's end. About 4.8 million cubic metres (6.2 million cubic yards) of concrete had been used. A further extension of the effort was hampered by the diversion of resources to other large fortification programs, starting with the construction of U-boat bunkers on the French coast from 1941. Once this was underway, Hitler ordered the first steps in the construction of a "new Westwall" to begin on the Atlantic Coast in December 1941, a program that was substantially enlarged in March 1942 under a new Führer directive as the Atlantikwall. This drew away most of the Organization Todt

TOP LEFT
The second Flak complex in Hamburg was built in the Wilhelmsburg district but was built in the simplified Typ 2 configuration as seen here in the case of Gefechtstürm VI. This complex was demolished in 1947. (NARA)

TOP RIGHT
The associated Leittürm VI in the Wilhelmsburg district of Hamburg was also completed in the simplified Typ 2 configuration. The Gefechtstürm VI can be seen in the background. (NARA)

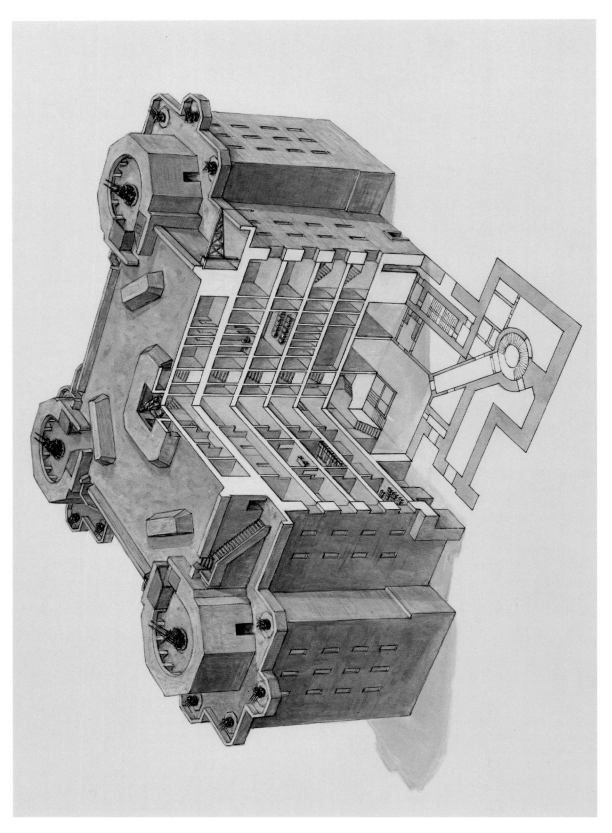

The final Flak tower to be constructed in 1944 was the Gefechtstürm VII in the Augarten, the popular Baroque gardens of Vienna. Two Vienna Flak complexes used the final Typ 3 configuration with simple round contours. The architect realized that the tower would be impossible to remove after the war, and planned to finish it in the style of the medieval Hohenstaufen castles with tiles and French marble. In the event, this decorative phase of construction never took place. Both Vienna Flak towers still remain, and the Augarten example is festooned with modern communication antenna and used for storage. (Wojciech Luczak)

resources that had been engaged in the civil defense effort in Germany; the Atlantikwall program eventually consumed about five times more concrete than that used in Germany for civil defense.

Berlin was complacent about the air-raid threat, because of the RAF's patchy performance in the first few years of the war. In 1940–41, the RAF targeted military objectives such as the railway network and oil production facilities. British bombers could not defend themselves in daylight against German fighters and were forced to resort to night bombing. However, navigation aids were so poor that bombing accuracy was abysmally low, and

D HOLY GHOST BUNKER, GEFECHTSSTAND IV, HAMBURG

This shows Gefechtsstand IV, part of the Heiligengeistfeld Typ 1 Flaktürm complex in Hamburg, and popularly known as the *Heiligengeistbunker* ("Holy Ghost bunker") by the local residents. This was a very substantial building, 70.5m (230ft) wide and 39m (130ft) high. The outer walls were 2.5m (8.2ft) thick while the roof was 3.5m (11.5ft). It followed the same Typ 1 pattern as the original Berlin Flak towers, with some minor architectural differences. This was the first tower to be built from the outset with the new 128mm Flak 40 Flakzwilling 40 (twin) heavy Flak guns. The secondary armament consisted of 20 20mm

Flakvierling 38 automatic cannon. The battery was manned by 1./414 schwere Flak-Abteilung (Türm), 3. Flak-Division and during 1942–45 it was credited with downing 50 Allied bombers. Fire direction data came from the nearby Leitstand IV, but the battery had its own Kommandogerät 40 optical gun director located in the square parapet at the centre of the roof. The Flaktürme cost about RM 45 million for each complex. The Hamburg tower was designed to accommodate 18,000 civilians, although it sometimes held as many as 60,000 under very crowded conditions.

precision targets were often missed. In February 1942 the RAF changed its mission to 'de-housing' the German industrial workforce by area attacks against German industrial cities. It took months before the RAF could mount raids of sufficient size to directly impact the German war industry.

By the spring of 1942, the RAF was beginning to emerge as the scourge of German cities. This became painfully evident in May 1942 when the RAF launched its first 'thousand-plane raid' against Cologne. Cologne had been on the list of priority cities under the Sofortprogramm. By the spring of 1942, 25 bunkers capable of accommodating 7,250 had been completed with 29 more still under construction. Splinter-proof shelters for a further 75,000 civilians, or about a tenth of the city's pre-war population of 760,000 people had been completed, mainly basement shelters and enclosed trenches. The Operation *Millennium* raid of May 30–31 delivered some 1,455 tons of bombs; casualties were about 460 dead and 5,025 wounded with more than 20,000 buildings damaged or destroyed. This was the last major raid until July 1943 when the RAF struck again. By 1944, the number of bunkers in Cologne had been increased to about 40 with a capacity of 12,000. Some of the capacity increase was accomplished by removing bunk beds and cramming in more people than the bunker's nominal capacity. In addition, the number of splinter-proof shelters had been doubled so that there were places for about 200,000. In general, the civil defenses in Cologne were deemed to be adequate considering the limited resources available. Total spending on the air-raid bunkers in Cologne had been RM 24 million and on all air-raid shelters about RM 39 million – rather less than the construction of a Berlin Flak tower complex.

Through the end of 1942, there were major raids on 19 German cities totalling 12,600 tons of bombs. While this was a major escalation in the scale of bombing compared to 1940–41, it was only a mild foretaste of the apocalypse that would descend on Germany over the next 30 months of war. Phase II (Welle II) of the Sofortprogramm began in 1942, aimed at fortifying 51 cities. A lack of resources cut this objective to only 30 cities. By this time, about 6 million cubic metres (8 million cubic yards) of concrete had been used and about 3,000 bunkers constructed. Phase III began in May 1943 but was the least productive of the three stages of the program due to the lack of construction resources.

A post-war survey of the city of Bockum provides a picture of the typical mixture of shelter types in a German city during the war. The survey was broken down between large industrial and public shelters, and privately constructed shelters.

Although shelter building continued unabated through the war, the diversion of so many construction resources to the Atlantikwall and other programs severely undermined the completion of the Sofortprogramm beyond the first phase. A variety of steps were introduced to streamline the scheme, including the 1942 Notausbauprogramm ("Emergency Construction Program"), which forbad the use of architectural detailing on the bunkers. The Sofortprogramm was largely abandoned by 1944, to be replaced by the Mindestbauprogramm ("Minimal Construction Program"), which, as the name implied, was aimed at reducing construction programs to only the most essential efforts. As mentioned in more detail below, this represented a shift from civil air-raid protection to factory protection.

The British air campaign against the Ruhr industrial region in the summer of 1943 marked another major escalation in the air campaign. The arrival of the new Lancaster bomber substantially increased the payload of the British force, and better tactics and navigation improved accuracy. The RAF had also learned important lessons from British experiences against the German Blitz of 1940 regarding the destructive forces of air attack. While pre-war tactics stressed the use of high-explosive bombs, the 1940 Battle of Britain made clear the paramount importance of fire in city destruction. RAF tactics shifted to a synergistic use of high-explosive and incendiaries, the high-explosive bombs to crack open the roofs of German urban structures and expose the wooden interior which were then ignited with small incendiary bomblets.

These tactics reached their horrifying crescendo in Hamburg in July 1943 when the RAF launched Operation *Gomorrah*. Hamburg had a normal population of 1.6 million and the city had 131 air-raid bunkers with a capacity of 10 percent of the population. There were also 49 deep tunnel shelters, 345 enclosed trench shelters, and about 1,800 basement shelters. In total, the city had a shelter capacity for about 600,000 plus more with overcrowding. The attacks began on the night of July 24, and continued for eight days and seven nights. On the night of July 27, the dry summer weather and the local wind conditions accelerated the combustion, creating the first known instance of man-made cyclonic

Air-raid shelters in Bockum		
Type	Number	Accommodations
Large bunkers	10	35,000
Deep bunkers	5	6,250
Tunnels	21	5,320
Hospital tunnels	4	4,100
Old mountain tunnels	4	5,100
Mine tunnels	370	24,000
Newly constructed tunnels	1,093	75,520
Industrial/Public shelter subtotal	*1,507*	*155,290*
Basement shelters	10,700	131,840
Large enclosed trenches	62	4,510
Shelters in buildings and schools	144	25,210
Private enclosed trenches	140	5,540
Private shelter subtotal	*11,046*	*167,100*
Total	12,553	322,390

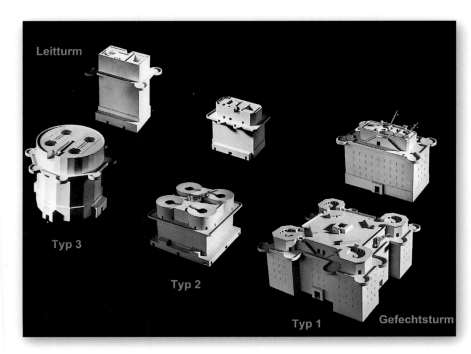

Leitturm

Typ 3

Typ 2

Typ 1 Gefechtsturm

This illustration compares the three generations of the *Flakturme* based on the architectural models prepared by the office of Prof. Friedrich Tamms. The gun towers (*Gefechtstürm*) are shown in the foreground, and the fire-control (*Leitstand*) in the background.

firestorms. This single night attack incinerated an area of about 21 square kilometres (8 square miles) and was responsible for the majority of the 42,000 deaths and 37,000 serious injuries caused by the operation. The basement shelters were especially vulnerable to the firestorms since they caused numerous building collapses and the occupants were asphyxiated by fumes or lack of oxygen. The small enclosed trench shelters were likewise vulnerable. The larger air-raid bunkers offered more reliable protection, if for no other reason than that they were often isolated from other buildings, which reduced the nearby stock of combustible materials. The vulnerability of the basement shelters and the better protection offered by the bunkers led to gross overcrowding. One Hamburg bunker designed for 18,000, was regularly occupied by more than 60,000 people.

The lessons of Hamburg had an impact elsewhere. By 1944–45, bunkers and bomb-proof tunnels in the major German cities had a nominal capacity to house about 15 percent of their population, but in actual circumstances, overcrowding allowed them to increase their capacity five-fold and to accommodate as much as 75 percent of the population. The ventilation systems in the bunkers could not compensate for this volume of people and during warmer weather, the internal temperatures in the bunkers could reach 50°C (120°F), which caused serious medical problems for its temporary inhabitants. Nevertheless, they provided a more secure refuge than the improvised basement shelters.

Aside from overcrowding, the bunkers also proved to be increasingly vulnerable to the heavier bombs being dropped by the RAF. The bunkers built in 1940–41 with the 1.4m-thick (4.6ft) roofs were proof only against 250kg (500lb) bombs, at a time when the Lancaster bombers had begun to drop 2- and 4-ton bombs. A variety of improvised solutions were attempted such as "elastic roofs," which consisted of a thick layer of straw on the existing roof and a further layer of concrete slabs above it. This was intended

Pre-fabricated BWS (*Brandwachenstände*, or fire warden posts) were manufactured in the thousands. Some early BWS manufactured in the 1930s were constructed of steel like this example, currently preserved at the Overloon Museum in the Netherlands. Once steel became scarce in the civilian economy, concrete became the preferred material. (Author)

E LEITTÜRM I, 1. FLAK-DIVISION, BERLIN

The fire control towers of the Berlin Flak bunkers have not attracted as much attention as the larger gun towers. The first of these was Leittürm I, built in the Tiergarten at the Berlin Zoo. Codenamed *Bär* A ("Bear A"), its primary role was to provide fire direction for the gun tower. On the roof was a FuSE 65 Würzburg-Riese surveillance radar, as well as a smaller FuMG 39T fire control radar and a Kommandogerät 40 gun director. The "sparrow's nests" in the control towers were supposed to be armed with the 50mm Maschinenflak 41 automatic cannon, but when this failed to enter serial production, the towers received the 20mm Flakvierling 38. The Zoo Bunker towers were painted

dark green, but other Flak towers appear to have been painted in dark grey. This L-Türm served as the command post of the 1. Flak Division during the war. The Berlin tower guns were manned by schwere Flak-Abteilung 123 (T), Flak-Regiment 172, under Oberstleutnant Karl Hoffmann. During the final siege of Berlin in May 1945, the Zoo towers were the scene of considerable fighting with the Red Army, and nearly 30,000 civilians sheltered in both towers. The Leitturm I surrendered at 0500hrs on May 2, 1945 and it was demolished by British engineers on June 28, 1947. It is now the site of the bird preserve island in the Berlin Zoo.

This common type of concrete BWS was manufactured by the Dywidag Betonwerke in Cossebaude near Dresden. It weighed 3,240kg and cost RM 430 to RM 480. When the Allied armies entered Germany, they were often used as improvised pillboxes like this example captured after the fighting in Eschwiller in December 1944. (NARA)

to detonate the bomb before it reached the main structure and dissipate some of its energy, but Luftwaffe officials were sceptical of the practice and banned it in late 1944 as ineffective.

Germany's civil defense shelter program was surprisingly effective in reducing the number of civilian losses. Total German civilian casualties to the Allied bombing campaign were at least 305,000 killed and 780,000 wounded; records for the final months of the war are lacking and so the casualty figures were undoubtedly higher. While these figures are quite substantial, the German civil defense effort significantly limited these totals. Much of the credit for this must be given to local municipal governments since Hitler showed little enthusiasm for the air-raid shelter program beyond a few hallmark structures such as the great Flak towers. The success or failure of the civil defense infrastructure largely depended on local governments and most did a credible job in spite of the severe restrictions on construction resources. Hitler expected that the Luftwaffe would prove to be as effective in air defense as the RAF had been during the 1940 Battle of Britain. However, Britain had invested far more in heavy bomber technology, and neither German Flak nor fighter aircraft proved sufficient especially once the USAAF added its substantial power to the air battles. If Berlin had better anticipated the Allied air threat, greater efforts at civilian air defense could have taken place in 1942–43 by using the construction resources that were wasted on building the misguided Atlantikwall.

DARK WORLD: UNDERGROUND FORTIFIED FACTORIES

Battle of the factories

In the autumn of 1943, the US Army Air Force launched Operation *Pointblank*, an air campaign to cripple the German fighter force by striking at its aircraft plants using precision daylight bomber attacks. This was a fundamental change from the British practice of night bombing the cities. The *Pointblank* campaign started slowly with a series of costly raids on the ball-bearing industry around Schweinfurt in October 1943. By January–February 1944, the enlarged US Strategic Air Forces (USSTAF) launched a series of very effective raids against German aircraft assembly plants. Although the attacks did not stop German aircraft production, the devastation greatly worried Berlin.

Aside from the air-raid shelter program connected with the Sofortprogramm, the German armament factories were not fortified until

The Valentin bunker at Farge on the Weser River outside Bremen was the first large bunker factory started in Germany in 1943 and was intended for the construction of the revolutionary new Type XXI U-boat. The bunker was hit by an RAF bomber attack on 27 March 1945 and the 4.5m-thick (14.5ft) roof was penetrated in two locations by "Grand Slam" heavy bombs. (NARA)

1944. Some passive defensive steps were taken, such as camouflage, the erection of decoy targets, and the creation of Luftwaffe smoke detachments to obscure industrial areas from precision bombing. However, these measures are largely outside the scope of this book.

The Ministry of Armaments and War Production (Reichsministerium für Rüstung und Kriegsproduktion) under Albert Speer had anticipated the vulnerability of the factories to air attack, and had already considered dispersing the aviation industry to make it less vulnerable. As early as 1941, Focke-Wulf began a modest, independent program to disperse its activities from its main plant in Bremen after an RAF raid. The air ministry studied an industry-wide dispersal plan in 1942, but it was shelved due to the negative impact it would have on output. As a first step, firms were encouraged to spread out their resources into neighbouring towns. Early in the war, some firms such as Messerschmitt, felt that the location of their plants in south-eastern Germany at Augsburg and Regensburg would keep them out of reach of British bombers; by late 1943 it was clear that this had been short-sighted. The instructions for a dispersal program were delayed until the last minute, and not issued until February 1944 after the USSTAF had begun its *Pointblank* attacks. The plan ordered the dispersion of the 27 main airplane plants into 729 small plants and the 59 aircraft engine plants to 249 locations.

From the initial American raids in February–March 1944, it became evident that the bombing attacks were more destructive of the factory buildings than the large machine tools within the buildings. As a result, in April 1944, Speer ordered the start of a factory fortification program as a temporary expedient until the

This is one of the entrances to the Lachs tunnel factory that was bored into an old porcelain sand mine near Kahla. Officially called the Flugzeugwerke Reichsmarschall Hermann Göring, only 27 Me-262 fighters were completed there before the end of the war. (NARA)

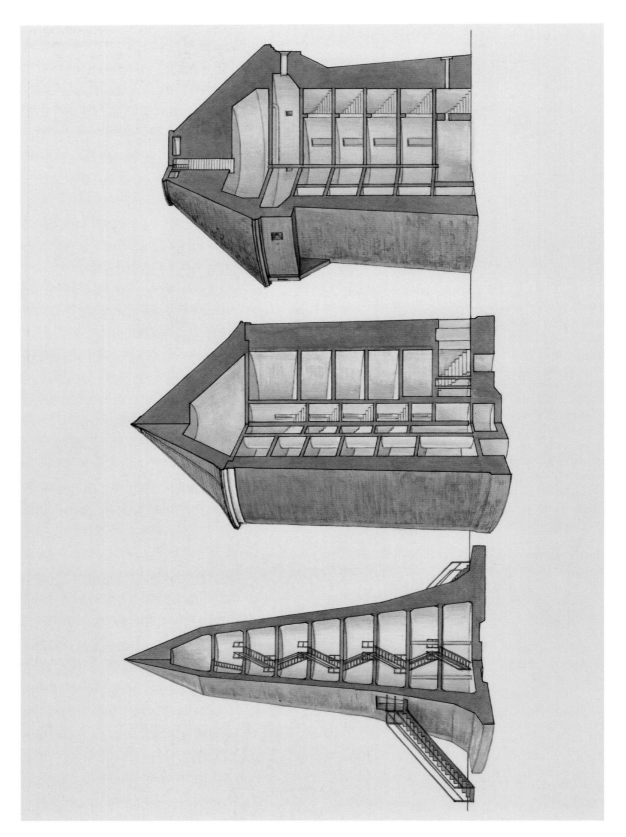

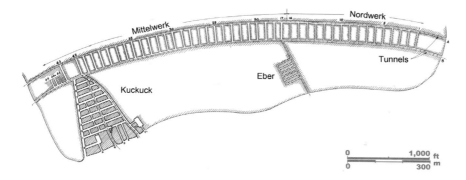

The Nordhausen underground complex in the Hart Mountains contained four separate factories, the Mittelwerk V-1 and V-2 missile assembly plant, the Nordwerk aviation plant, the Kuckuck gasoline plant, and the Eber liquid oxygen plant. This map is based on a post-war US survey. (NARA)

dispersion program could take effect. Major machine tools had blast walls erected around them to protect them in the event that bombs detonated nearby. A ministry study later concluded that the early raids against factories without blast-walls led to damage of 47 percent of the machine tools, while this was reduced to only about 13.5 percent once blast-walls were installed.

There were at least four avenues for dispersion of the aircraft plants: to smaller plants around Germany and occupied Europe; to improvised assembly works in forested areas; to underground locations such as caves, mines and railroad tunnels; or to custom-built underground factories. Messerschmitt was one of the most enthusiastic advocates of forest plants and created over a dozen such facilities in Bavaria. Highest priority went to the new Me-262 jet fighter. After the main plant at Augsburg was bombed on February 25–26, the Me-262 assembly work was temporarily dispersed to Leipheim air base. During March 1944, the assembly was shifted to a nearby forest factory (Waldwerk) under the codename Waldwerk Kuno 1, using a nearby stretch of autobahn A8 as the runway for completed aircraft. A series of these dispersed forest factories were added over the next few months, including Waldwerk Hasenbühl near Schwäbisch Hall in May 1944, Kuno II

F   LUFTSCHUTZE-TÜRME

These cross-sectional drawings show three of the many types of air-raid shelter towers. They differ considerably in detail and design, in part due to German patent laws that encouraged architectural firms to vary the configuration in order to secure patent rights. In most cases, these firms offered a basic design in several sizes for more or fewer occupants. Filling the building as quickly as possible during an air-raid was one of several important criteria in building design. The earliest designs such as Winkel used a simple central staircase, which limited the speed of filling the building, since slower people and those running out of breath at the upper floors would slow the loading process.

To the left is the classic LS-Türm der Bauart Winkel Typ 1c. The Winkel buildings were categorized in two fashions. The type designation indicated the capacity, so Typ 1 could hold 400 people, Typ 2 some 315 people, etc. This is a second-generation Typ 1c; the earliest designs had two sub-basement levels but this configuration was simpler to construct with all nine levels above the surface. The Luftwaffe also issued its own designations depending on the configuration, so the one shown here is the RL 3-40/5 with the steeply angled *Zuckerhut-Form* ("sugerloaf"), while the RL 3-40/1

design used a shallower cone roof. Winkel towers such as this one had two access points on different levels so that it could be quickly filled.

The LS-Türm der Bauart Zombeck seen here in the centre took another approach to loading. Although it had a central staircase tower, it did not have conventional flat floors but rather a single, rotating screw configuration. So people could use the central staircase, portions of the crowd could be siphoned off at each "floor" and continue the journey upward inside the main body of the tower until all the places were filled. As in the case of the Winkel towers, the Zombeck towers came in different sizes, so the B1 type shown here had a capacity for 500 people, a height of 22.2m (73ft), and 5.5 windings; the B2 had a capacity of 450, a height of 21m (69ft) and 5 windings, etc. External design features also varied, with many towers left in the original cast-concrete, but some having architectural veneers of brick and roofing tiles as seen here.

The LS-Türm der Bauart Dietel was a larger and squatter design that could accommodate 1,000 people. It employed a set of broad stairs around the central core to speed loading. The flat roof encouraged local units to mount 20mm Flak cannon on the roof, even though that was not authorized.

The Nordwerk aviation plant in the older northern section of the Nordhausen complex was used for aircraft assembly, including the construction of He-162 Volksjäger jet fighters as seen here. The plan was to construct 2,000 fighters here per month once the tunnels were finished. (NARA)

in September 1944, Waldwerk Stauffen near Obertraubling in December 1944, and Waldwerk Neuberg/Donau in January 1945. The process was to disperse the sub-assembly plants to scattered locations or underground, while conducting the final assemblies in the forest factories. Messerschmitt later compared the relative costs of one of their forest factories in Gauting against a tunnel plant in Kematen and found that the forest plant took only two months and cost RM 0.7 million for a 1,200 worker facility, while the Kematen plant took eight months and RM 4.1 million for a plant half the size with only 730 workers. None of the forest plants were discovered by Allied intelligence during the war and none were bombed intentionally.

The use of caves, mines, and tunnels for aviation industry dispersal was not a new idea, and had already been tried in France in 1943–44 in connection with the deployment of V-weapons, especially the V-1 (Fiesler Fi-103) cruise missile. Tunnels and mine-shafts were used as bomb-proof ordnance depots for the missiles. The most elaborate underground facility for the V-weapons was the massive Mittelwerk complex in the tunnels outside Nordhausen. The original plan had been to start production of the advanced A-4 (V-2) ballistic missile at a conventional plant near the Peenemünde missile test site. On the night of August 17–18, 1943, the RAF launched the Operation *Hydra* raid against the secret Peenemünde facility, causing extensive damage. The vulnerability of this site led to a decision on 24 September 1943 to shift production to the new government-controlled Mittelwerk corporation, which was building an underground plant near Nordhausen on the basis of an existing tunnel system previously used to store fuel. To extend the tunnels sufficiently to create an underground factory required an enormous amount of work, and much of the excavation was carried out by inmates from Work Camp Dora, a sub-camp of the nearby Buchenwald concentration camp. The use of forced labour secured the role of Himmler's SS in the underground factories programs, since the SS controlled the camps and their slave labour force. SS management of the underground program was assumed by Brigadeführer Hans Kammler, a civil engineer who headed the construction department of the SS economic and administrative main office, and who had played a prominent role in the construction of the ultra-secret death camps at Auschwitz-Birkenau, Majdanek, and Belzec. Due to the appalling work and living conditions, the death rate among the Mittelwerk prisoners was horrific, with over 3,000 dead by January 1944. The Mittelwerk complex helped establish a pattern for the use of underground facilities for high-priority armaments programs as well as the increasing role of the SS in these programs.

Following the February 1944 dispersal order, Speer established a special agency to search for suitable tunnels and caves in Germany. Himmler also became enamoured of the underground factory idea after discovering a vast complex of tunnels and chambers under the city of Warsaw. So the SS established its own program to search for suitable underground factory locations, with a special emphasis on old underground city locations in Germany and the occupied territories. Many aircraft plants were reluctant to use tunnels and mines because of humidity and ventilation problems, but as Allied bombing raids against the industry continued, more and more plants began to move their facilities underground. In general, underground mine and tunnel dispersal was regarded more as an act of desperation than an effective industrial policy. Allied intelligence after the war discovered at least 340 major German underground installations, including both the improvised use of existing mines and tunnels, as well as newly constructed tunnels.

The best-known role of the Nordhausen complex was the construction of the A-4 (V-2) ballistic missile and Fi-103 (V-1) cruise missile in the Mittelwerk section of the complex. This is an A-4 missile fuselage prior to installation of the rocket engine. (NARA)

The German aviation industry was successful in dispersing the industry to reduce its vulnerability to bombing attacks, but dispersion came at a steep cost. Plant dispersion made the industry more vulnerable to disruption in the transportation network since sub-components had to be shipped by rail or canal to other locations, and Allied attacks on the transportation network later in the war created significant problems. Dispersion diluted the supervisory and technical talent in the industry and led to the rapid decline in aircraft quality in the later months of the war that severely affected the actual combat utility of the aircraft. The loss of aircraft due to mechanical malfunctions increased alarmingly. Dispersion required a larger workforce at a time when labour shortages were endemic and forced the industry to make greater use of foreign forced labour which led to sabotage problems, further depreciating aircraft quality.

Speer and the aircraft industry leaders recognized the shortcomings of a dispersed production structure, and hoped in the longer-term to create massive underground factories. Messerschmitt intended to shift much of its high-priority Me-262 jet fighter production from the improvised forest factories to custom-built underground factories. The B8 Bergkristall underground plant, codenamed Esche II, near Sankt Georgen was one of the largest of the tunnel complexes built during the war using slave labour from the nearby Mauthausen-Gusen concentration camp. The tunnels were about 10km (6 miles) in length and were completely reinforced with concrete. Construction began in March 1944, and was almost complete by the end of the war. Even though not fully finished, the Esche II factory turned out 987 Me-262 fuselages. Another underground facility was tunnelled into an old porcelain sand mine near Kahla outside Weimar. Codenamed *Lachs* ("salmon"), it was better known as the Flugzeugwerke Reichsmarschall Hermann Göring (REIMAHG), but only 27 Me-262 fighters were completed there before the end of the war. To support the jet fighter program, Junkers was assigned the underground Malachit plant near Langenstein, which had an objective of producing 1,000 jet engines monthly; production only started in April 1945. Daimler-Benz shifted a major portion of its aviation engine

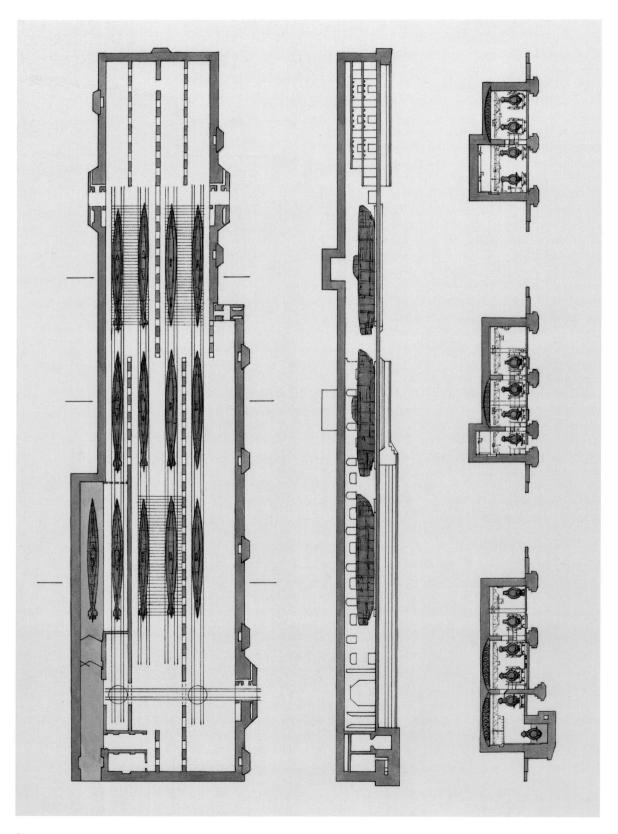

plants to a new Neckar-Elms underground plant built by the SS, codenamed *Goldfisch*. The large underground tunnel plants had considerable potential because they were largely bomb-proof. A post-war British survey of the sites concluded that they offered enough overhead protection that it made "an air attack even with the largest (Grand Slam) penetrating bombs unprofitable." However, the survey also noted that the German designs were not sufficiently protected near the entrances. In the event, the main drawback to the tunnel factories was the amount of time needed to construct them, and few were ready before the war ended.

Dispersion of the aircraft plants to camouflaged locations was the simplest approach to reducing the vulnerability of the aircraft factories. This is a view of one of the camouflaged assembly sheds at Waldwerk Stauffen near Obertraubling. A partially completed Me-262 jet fighter can be seen to the left. (NARA)

Factory bunkers

Tunnels were impractical in some areas of Germany due to terrain, and an alternative was the use of bunkers that were large enough to contain entire factories. The inspiration for these factories came from the U-Boat bunkers and V-weapon heavy launch sites built earlier in the war by Organization Todt. The U-Boat bunkers were constructed at French, Norwegian, and German ports from 1941, and were inspired by structures that had been built during World War I by the Kriegsmarine to protect U-Boats in Bruges, Belgium on the North Sea coast.[3] Throughout much of the war, the U-boat bunkers, with their thick reinforced concrete roofs, were virtually invulnerable to bomber attack. Extensive Allied bomber attacks on German U-boat yards in 1943 delayed production of the new Type XXI boat, and as a result, the massive "Valentin" bunker factory for assembling the new design entered construction in 1943 on the Weser River at Farge outside Bremen. The facility was struck by Allied bombers in late March 1945 and British heavy bombs penetrated the roof, which prevented its completion even though it was almost 90 percent done.

---

3 Gordon Williamson, *U-Boat Bases and Bunkers 1941–45*, (Osprey Fortress 3, 2003)

G BUNKER VALENTIN U-BOAT FACTORY, FARGE

Plans to build fortified plants for submarine construction took shape in November 1942 with a scheme to construct a facility codenamed *Hornisse* ("hornet") for the Deschimag yard in Bremen, *Wespe* ("wasp") for the Blohm & Voss yard, and the Valentin factory for Bremer Vulkan in Vegesack. With the advent of revolutionary new modular Type XXI submarine the plans were altered so that Hornisse and Wespe would be used to manufacture sections of the submarine, and then the sections would be shipped to Valentin for final assembly. In the event, neither Hornisse nor Wespe were ever started and the site for the Valentin fortified factory was shifted to Farge, about 8km (5 miles) north of Vegesack on the Weser River.

This was the largest bunker built in Germany during the war, the only larger structure in Europe being the U-boat shelters in Brest, France. Construction consumed about a million tons of gravel and sand, 132,000 tons of cement, 500,000 cubic metres of concrete (650,000 cubic yards), and 20,000 tons of steel. About 12,000 forced labourers were used in its construction of whom about 1,700 died from malnutrition or execution. The building originally had a roof 4.5m (15ft) thick, but this was supposed to be increased to 10m (33ft) due to the expectation that Allied bombs were improving. The walls were originally 4.5m (15ft) thick, later increased to 7m (23ft). Valentin was 420m (1,375ft) long, 95m (315ft) wide and 30m (95ft) high. It had four assembly tracks running most of the length of the building so that up to a dozen submarines could be assembled at one time. The building was about 90 percent complete when it was struck by an RAF raid on March 27, 1945. Two 10-ton "Grand Slam" bombs damaged two sections of the roof, which was the original 4.5m (15ft) thickness; a post-war Allied assessment concluded that had they been strengthened as planned, they would have resisted these bombs.

Besides the U-boat bunkers, Organization Todt had also been working on a series of bunkers to house the V-weapon force in France.[4] The first of these *Wasserwerk* ("reservoir") sites were subjected to RAF air raids in August 1943 that managed to penetrate the Kraftwerk Nordwest bunker near Watten on August 27, 1943 even though the roof was protected by a reinforced concrete roof 5m (16ft) thick. The failure of this bunker to resist the new British super-heavy bombs led to several innovations in heavy bunker construction, including a new construction method dubbed "*Erdschalung*" ("earth mould") in which the roof of the building was built on a temporary earthen core to prevent bomb penetration during construction, and then the building interior was hollowed out after the concrete had cured. This was first used at the improved V-weapon Wasserwerk site at Siracourt, which was approaching completion when overrun after the D-Day landings in Normandy in the summer of 1944.

In March 1944, Organization Todt initiated Project *Ringeltaube* ("wood pigeon") to construct aviation factory bunkers using the techniques earlier developed for the Wasserwerk bunkers. Eight large factories were authorized in March 1944 for Messerschmitt, mainly in the Landsberg area south of Augsburg, with a capacity of 1,000 to 1,200 Me-262 jet fighters per month. The original plan called for a large arched building like the Siracourt V-weapons site. A lack of labour and resources trimmed the number of sites from eight to four. The factory bunkers were constructed by using a core of gravel graded to the appropriate shape after which the arch was poured in sections. After the concrete had hardened in one section, the gravel fill was excavated and in the meantime, construction proceeded to the next section. The massive concrete hangar represented only the outer layer of the bunker. The interior contained a separate concrete factory building, with the space between the arch and the building serving for ventilation. The interior factory building was built largely of pre-cast components from the new Rudolph II plant in nearby Utting. The height of the interior building depended on the local topography. The Weingut I (Vineyard I) bunker at Mühldorf had an eight-storey interior building, while the Weingut II plant near Landsberg was limited to five-storeys due to a higher water table in the area. Although the construction began with conventional labour sources, Project *Ringeltaube*

---

[4] Steven Zaloga, *German V-Weapon Sites 1943–45*, (Osprey Fortress 72, 2008)

soon began to use forced labour to speed up the programs, mainly from Dachau and its satellite camps. Of the 30,000 labourers working on the Landsberg site, about 14,500 died from malnutrition and abuse. These bunkers were quite expensive to construct, each costing about RM 20 million. Although nearing completion, none was ready to manufacture aircraft by the end of the war.

Operation *Desert*

In the wake of the attack on the aircraft industry in January–April 1944, the USSTAF began to expand its targeting in May 1944 to the German fuel hydrogenation plants: the factories that made synthetic, high-octane fuel for the Luftwaffe. These raids, combined with the loss of the Romanian oil fields to the Red Army in the summer of 1944, threatened to shut down the Wehrmacht by starving it of fuel. As a result, Hitler appointed one of Speer's associates, Edmund Geilenberg, as Generalkommissar für Sofortmaßnahmen ("General Commissioner for Emergency Measures") on May 31, 1944. The ensuing Operation *Desert* (Unternehmen Wüste) was an effort to fortify the existing fuel refineries against air attack, disperse the most vulnerable plants, and begin to create underground and bunker facilities to shield the fuel industry from air attack. The June 21, 1944 instructions ordered the creation of *Hydrierfestungen* ("hydrogenation fortresses") at 15 of the most vulnerable plants. This included the transfer of over 2,000 Flak guns to the sites, as well as the addition of blast walls and other protective measures.

Besides the reinforcement of existing plants, the Geilenberg program envisioned the creation of 140 new plants at a staggering cost of RM 1.4 billion. The industry preferred to locate as many of the new plants underground or in bunkers as was feasible. Since this would triple the cost of the program, all but 21 high-priority facilities were built as small, dispersed surface plants. At the heart of the scheme was the creation of seven new underground hydrogenation plants and one bunker plant under the codename *Schwalbe* ("swallow"). An additional hydrogenation plant, codenamed *Kuckuck* ("cuckoo") was to be built inside one of the sections of the Nordhausen underground tunnel network. In total, some 18 new aviation fuel plants were planned for completion between February 1945 and July 1946. The motor gasoline industry was to be revived by creating 41 dispersed plants consisting mainly of small distillation installations in forests, underground or in the ruins of old factories. Since lubricating oil plants could not be easily dispersed, eight new plants were planned, six of which were underground; they were codenamed *Dachs* ("badger"), with completion planned for May 1945 to May 1946. Additional dispersed plants were planned for diesel fuel. One of the most outlandish schemes under Operation *Desert* was to cover a mountain in a thick coat of concrete, and then excavate the interior to create a massive bunker; this scheme never proceeded beyond the planning stage. In the event, Operation *Desert* was an expensive

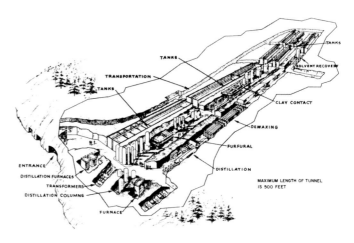

One of the few underground fuel plants nearly to reach completion was the Dachs 1 lubrication oil plant near Porta. Due to the nature of the lubrication oil production process, the entire plant had to be constructed as a unified system in a series of reinforced tunnels as seen in this post-war US intelligence report. (NARA)

failure, with a high human cost because of the callous abuse of slave labour. None of the new hydrogenation plants were completed before the end of the war, though Dachs 1 near Porta was nearly finished.

The fortification of Germany's military industries from bomber attack was delayed too long. The RAF's focus on city attacks in 1941–43 lulled Berlin into thinking that the factories were relatively safe. When the USAAF began a dedicated campaign in early 1944 against the aircraft industry and then the fuel industry, it was too late for an effective response. The March 1944 factory dispersion plan was a temporary expedient that prevented the immediate collapse of the military industries, but the relentless Allied bomber campaigns in late 1944 and early 1945 led to a catastrophic collapse in industrial production before the tunnel factories and bunker factories reached the production stage.

THE SITES TODAY

In spite of their failures, the German air defense construction effort was the source of considerable fascination to British and American military planners. The German bunker designs, both for civil defense and factory defense, were amongst the most sophisticated in the world. The bold schemes to build entire factories under heavy concrete were studied very carefully by Allied engineers who saw them as critical forerunners of the underground defenses that would be needed in the age of nuclear weapons. German construction techniques served as the inspiration for later American, British, and Soviet Cold War defenses.

Fortified air raid shelters were banned by the Occupation authorities in 1945–47, but in practice, few shelters were razed because they fulfilled the immediate need for housing in the devastated cities. The Occupation authorities blew up a few prominent fortified bunkers, but this was undertaken partly as a symbolic effort, and partly as a means of examining the protective features of the structures.

The Flak towers are a good example of the erratic demolition efforts. The French army's attempts to demolish the Humboldthain G-Stand in Berlin led to a partial collapse. Rather than waste time and expense removing it entirely, the collapsed portion was covered with debris and earth; a side of the structure still remains today. The Friedrichshain bunker was blown up by British Royal Engineers, but the several explosions only managed to partially collapse the building. Due to its location in the Berlin Zoo garden, the German government spent over a decade clearing up the debris, finally trucking away half a million

H WEINGUT I FORTIFIED AVIATION PLANT, MÜHLDORF

The Weingut I fortified factory was one of four that started construction around Munich under Project Ringeltaube to manufacture the Messerschmitt Me-262 jet fighter. This enormous arch was 5m (16ft) thick, 360m (1,180ft) long, and 85m (280ft) wide; the anticipated cost was RM 20.2 million. About 10,000 forced labourers from the nearby Mühldorf concentration camp performed most of the work. The Weingut I plant was supposed to contain an eight-storey, concrete factory building inside it; the Weingut 2 plant in nearby Landsberg had only a five-story building due to a higher water-table in the area. The drawing here shows the intended design of the building, with a set of ten concrete mushroom openings for exhaust and air intake. The plan was to enclose the plant in earth about two-fifths up the side of the building, and to cover the rest with a thin coat of earth to grow plants and other vegetation for camouflage, with only the air intakes left exposed. Both ends of the building would be sealed by a 5m (16ft) wall, except for a set of large doors, not shown here. The planned completion of the building was not until 1946, and so only seven of the planned 12 sections were completed by April 1945 when construction was halted by the advance of US Army units nearby. Some elements such as the intake/exhaust ports were not started and so are not well documented.

The smaller Leittürm I in the Tiergarten was the first portion of the Zoo Bunker complex in Berlin to be demolished on June 28, 1947. The radars can still be seen in position on the top of the structure. (NARA)

cubic metres of rubble in 1957; the remains of the foundation were not removed until 1969. Some of the Flak towers in Hamburg and Vienna still exist. The massive Valentin submarine bunker near Bremen was used after the war by the RAF and USAAF as a test ground for penetration bombs. In 1960, it was taken over by the Bundesmarine as a storage facility. There were several plans to raze the building, but its enormous size and tough construction made this too expensive. It was finally retired from government use in 2010 and in 2011, when the Bremen government announced plans to create a memorial museum there to commemorate the nearly 2,000 forced labourers who died during its construction.

In contrast to the Flak towers, most other German Flak positions were temporary field works and so disappeared after the war. There are still remnants of gun-pits at many locations, especially those in more remote locations and those made partially from brick or concrete. The concrete Atlantikwall Flak displacements, especially those in the Netherlands and Belgium, are still present in abundance along the coast.

German air-raid bunkers were often used as temporary housing after the war due to the widespread devastation in German cities. Over the years, many were removed as ugly and obnoxious reminders of the hostilities. But the bunkers were so durable that many were simply left in place. Some have been converted to other uses such as storage and museums. The books listed in the next section include a number of archaeological guides to several German cities that catalogue the remaining air defense structures. There are thousands of buildings still in existence, though the numbers diminish year by year.

FURTHER READING

There is an extensive literature on German air defense efforts in World War II, though it is disjointed and has some noticeable gaps. Flak is amply documented, most notably the Westermann study. However, the aspect of Flak of most interest here, its fortified deployment, is not well covered in published accounts. I found ample documentation in archival records, especially the extensive collection of Luftwaffe manuals in Record Group 242 at the US National Archives and Records Administration (NARA II) in College Park, Maryland. Histories of the development of Luftwaffe air defense radar and the related issue of integrated air defense systems are not well represented in English except for the Svejgaard accounts on Denmark, though there are some useful German studies.

The Hampe study provides the classic account of German civil air defense during the war, but the focus is institutional and there is relatively little detail on the air-raid shelter programs. There is no historical overview of German air-raid shelter development, though the US Strategic Bombing Survey (USSBS) reports provide a useful start. Some of the individual city studies are especially helpful; the Hamburg study provides an excellent background into the overall civil air defense organization as well as shelter construction. There is a growing literature on the air defense infrastructure in various German cities, evidence of the recent upsurge in interest in Germany in local urban archaeology and the rise of the "Dark World" (*Dunkle Welten*) movement in Berlin of underground urban explorers. There are a number of German enthusiast groups studying the wartime shelters such as the Igel (Interessengemeinschaft zur Erforschung von Luftschutzbauten – see www.luftschutz-bunker.de). In addition, the recent rise in German interest in the experience of German civilians during the 1940–45 bombing campaigns has led to a broad range of published accounts which deal tangentially with air-raid protection.

The fortified factory program of 1944–45 has largely escaped any coherent study, though the programs are covered from a variety of angles in various histories. Some accounts of German jet fighter development deal with the associated underground factory program, and there are a handful of specialized studies on individual plants such as Valentin. The historical field of Holocaust studies has led to a great deal of research into the SS concentration camps, and the intimate connection between underground factory construction and the use of slave labour has uncovered a growing amount of information.

In August 1947, 338 Construction Squadron, Royal Engineers, set about preparing Gefechtstürm I of the Zoo Bunker complex for demolition. The first two detonations on August 30 and September 27, 1947 damaged the building, but failed to bring it down. A third attempt on July 30, 1948 finally collapsed the structure as seen here. The majority of the rubble was finally taken away in 1955–57, but the foundations were not removed until 1969. The hippopotamus enclosure of Berlin Zoo is now located on the site of the G-Türm. (NARA)

Government reports

Aircraft Division Industry Report, (US Strategic Bombing Survey, Aircraft Division Report E-4: 1947)

Ausbildungsvorschrift für die Flakartillerie: Feldbefestigungen der Flakartillerie L.Dv.400/11a, (Luftwaffe: March 1940)

Ausbildungsvorschrift für die Flakartillerie: Stellungs- und Befestigungsbau der Flakartillerie L.Dv.400/11a, (Luftwaffe: October 1943)

Civilian Defense Division Final Report, (US Strategic Bombing Survey, Civilian Defense Division Report: 1947)

Cologne Field Report, (US Strategic Bombing Survey, Civilian Defense Division Report E-41: 1947)

Comparative Test of the Effectiveness of Large Bombs Against Reinforced Concrete Structures; Anglo-American Bomb Tests 'Project Ruby', (Air Proving Ground, Eglin AFB: 1946)

The Effects of Strategic Bombing on the German War Economy, (US Strategic Bombing Survey Overall Effects Division Report E-3: 1945)

The sturdy construction of the large air-raid bunkers has made their demolition prohibitively expensive. This example in the port city of Danzig (today Gdansk, Poland) was a fairly typical 1943 example, with a prominent air ventilation structure on the roof. It was built in the Old Town district near the harbour, currently at Ulica Olejarnia 2A. It was somewhat different from many other public shelters because it also housed a Luftwaffe command post, and had Flak guns mounted on the roof, a configuration generally frowned on elsewhere. (Wojciech Luczak)

Fire Raids on German Cities, (US Strategic Bombing Survey Physical Damage Division Report E-193: 1947)

Flak Defenses of Strategic Targets in Southern Germany, (AAF Evaluation Board-ETO: 1947)

The 14th Flak Division: Its history, organization, layout and role in the defense of central Germany, (CSDIC: 1945)

The German Flak Effort Throughout the War, (US Strategic Bombing Survey, Military Analysis Division Memo: 1947)

The German Passive Air Defense Services, (Historical Division, US Air Force: 1957)

German Underground Installations, (Joint Intelligence Objectives Agency: 1945)

Hamburg Field Report, (US Strategic Bombing Survey, Civilian Defense Division Report E-44: 1947)

Public Air Raid Shelters in Germany, (US Strategic Bombing Survey Physical Damage Division Report E-154: 1947)

Underground and Dispersal Plants in Greater Germany, (US Strategic Bombing Survey Oil Division Report E-112: 1947)

Underground Factories in Germany, (Combined Intelligence Objectives Sub-Committee: 1945)

Books

Dietmar Arnold, Ingmar Arnold, Frieder Salm, *Dunkle Welten: Bunker, Tunnel und Gewölbe unter Berlin*, (Ch.Links: 2010)

Beck, Earl, *Under the Bombs: The German Home Front 1942–45*, (University Press of Kentucky, 1998)

Buggeln, Marc, *Bunker Valentin*, (Temmen, 2010)

Foedrowitz, Michael, *Einmannbunker: Splitterschutzbauten und Brandwachenstände*, (Motorbuch, 1998)

——, *Luftschutztürme der Bauart Winkel in Deutschland 1936 bis heute*, (Podzun-Pallas, 1998)

——, *Luftschutztürme und ihre Bauarten 1934 bis heute*, (Podzun-Pallas, 1998)

——, *The Flak Towers in Berlin, Hamburg and Vienna 1940–1950*, (Schiffer, 1998)

——, *Bunkerwelten: Luftschutzanlagen in Norddeutschland*, (Dörfler, 2006)

Gleichmann, Marcus, & Bock, Karl-Heinz,*Düsenjäger über dem Walpersberg: Die Geschichte des unterirdischen Flugzeugwerekes REIMAHG bie Kahla/Thuringen*, (Heinrich Jung, 2009)

Gückelhorn, Wolfgang, *Die Koblenzer Luftschutzbunker im alliierten Bombenhagel*, (Helios: 2008)

Golücke, Friedhelm, *Schweinfurt und der strategische Luftkrieg 1943*, (Schöningh, 1977)

Hampe, Erich, *Der Zivile Luftschutz im Zweiten Weltkrieg*, (Bernard & Graefe, 1963)

Immekus, Andreas, *Militärische Anlagen in historischen Luftbildern: Flugabwehr*, (Büro Immekus, 2009)

Koch, Adalbert, *Die Geschichte der deutschen Flakartillerie 1935–1945*, (Podzun-Pallas, 1954)

Kuffner, Alexander, *Zeitreiseführer: Köln 1933–1945*, (Helios, 2009)

Lemke, Berd, *Luftschutz in Großbritannien und Deutschland 1923 bis 1939*, (Oldenbourg, 2004)

Littlejohn, David, *Defending the Reich*, (Bender, 2007)

Lowe, Keith, *Inferno: the Fiery Destruction of Hamburg 1943*, (Scribner, 2007)

Maehler, Wilfred, Michale Ide, *Luftschutz in Bochum*, (Diguprint, 2004)

Moorhouse, Roger, *Berlin at War*, (Basic Books, 2010)

Müller, Werner, *Die Geschütze, Ortungs- und Feuerleitgerte der schweren Flak*, (Podzun-Palls, 1988)

——, *Sound Locators, Fire Control Systems and Searchlights of the German Heavy Flak Units 1939–1945*, (Schiffer, 1998)

——, *Ground Radar Units of the Luftwaffe 1939–1945*, (Schiffer, 1998)

——, *The Heavy Flak Guns 1939–1945*, (Schiffer, 1990)

O'Brien, Andreas, Holger Raddatz, *Die verbunkerte Stadt: Luftschutzanlagen in Osnabrück un Umkreis*, (Books on Demand, 2009)

Price, Alfred, *Instruments of Darkness: The History of Electronic Warfare*, (Scribners, 1967)

Purpus, Elke, & Sellen, Günther, *Bunker in Köln*, (Klartext, 2006)

Sakkers, Hans, *Flaktürme*, (Fortress Books, 1998)

Schiller, Peter, et. al., *Die Bomber kamen bald jede Nacht: Luftschutz, Luftabwehr und Luftangriffe 1933/45 im Städedreieck Hamburg-Lübeck-Neumünster*, (Arbeitkreis Geschichte im Amt Trave-Land, 2009)

Schmal, Helga, & Selke, Tobias, *Bunker, Luftschutz und Luftschutzbau in Hamburg*, (Christians, 2001)

Svejgaard, Michael, *Der Luftnachrichten Dienst in Denmark 9 April 1940–5 May 1945*, (Gyges, 2003)

——, *The Kriegsmarine Command, Control and Reporting System, Bunkers and Electronic Systems in Denmark 9 April 1940–5 May 1945*, (Gyges, 2007)

Thiel, Reinhold, *Die Bremische Flugabwehr im Zweiten Weltkrieg*, (Hauschild Bremen, 1995)

Titsch, Markus, *Bunker im Wilhelmshaven*, (Brune-Mettcker, 2005)

Westermann, Edward, *Flak: German Anti-Aircraft Defenses 1941-1945*, (Univeristy Press of Kansas, 2001)

Willen, Susanne, *Der Kölner Architekt Hans Scuhhmacher: Sein Lebenswerk bis 1945*, (Köln, 1996)

INDEX